THE MONEY MAZE
AND YOUR PATH TO SUCCESS

THE MONEY MAZE
AND YOUR PATH TO SUCCESS

What all **Canadians Should Know**
About Managing Their Personal Finances

BOB TRASK

DISCLAIMER

This book is written by Bob Trask in his individual capacity and not as a registered representation of Raymond James Ltd. (RJL) or any of its affiliates. It expresses the opinions of the author and not necessarily those of Raymond James Ltd.

This book is provided as a general source of information and should not be considered personal investment advice or financial planning advice. It should not be construed as an offer or solicitation for the sale or purchase of any product and should not be considered tax advice.

We are not tax advisors and we recommend that clients seek independent advice from a professional advisor on tax-related matters.

We recommend any individual seek independent advice from an investment advisor prior to making any investment decisions and from a professional accountant concerning tax-related matters.

Statistics, factual data and other information are from sources RJL believes to be reliable but their accuracy cannot be guaranteed.

This book is furnished on the basis and understanding that Raymond James Ltd. or any of its affiliates are to be under no liability whatsoever in respect therefore.

This book may provide reference to third-party services. Raymond James Ltd. is not responsible for the availability of these external services, nor does Raymond James Ltd endorse, warrant or guarantee the products, services or information described or offered.

Commissions, trailing commissions, management fees and expenses all may be associated with mutual funds and exchange traded funds. Please read the prospectus before investing. Mutual funds and exchange traded funds are not guaranteed, their values change frequently and past performance may not be repeated.

Securities-related products and services are offered through Raymond James Ltd., Member-Canadian Investor Protection Fund Insurance products and services products and services are offered through Raymond James Financial Planning Ltd., which is not a Member-Canadian Investor Protection Fund.

ABOUT THE AUTHOR

Bob Trask has spent more than 25 years in the financial services industry. During his career he has been licensed to trade in stocks, bonds, mutual funds, exchange traded options and commodity futures. He has successfully completed the Canadian Securities Course and the Professional Financial Planning Course and has achieved the designation of Certified Investment Manager offered through the Canadian Securities Institute.

Bob strongly believes in the value of education when it comes to financial matters and in writing this book he addresses the many issues facing Canadians today. His experience in dealing with clients face to face and dealing with their concerns has given him an understanding of how emotions play a big role in decision making.

Bob lives in Saskatoon and is the proud father of two daughters, Brittany and Stephanie, who are pursuing their careers in engineering.

Copyright © 2013 by Robert Warren Trask
All rights reserved. No part of this publication may be reproduced in any form or by any means, electronic or mechanical, including photocopying, recording or any information storage and retrieval system without permission in writing from the publisher.

Published in 2013
by
Briste Press
702 – 311 6th Ave North
Saskatoon, Saskatchewan, Canada
S7K 7A9

Canadian Catalogue Publishing Data
Trask, Robert Warren, 1953 –
The Money Maze And Your Path To Success
ISBN: 978-0-9919473-0-0

Although the author has researched all sources to ensure accuracy and completeness of the information in this book, we assume inaccuracies, errors, omissions or inconsistency herein. This book is designed as a guide to help you through the process of managing your finances. The information in this document is not designed as personalized financial advice and should not be considered as such. Readers should consult the advice of the appropriate professionals before making any decisions regarding their personal finances.

Editor: Marli King
Cover Design: Steven Plummer
Typesetting: Steven Plummer

Printed in the United States

Table of Contents

Preface 9

SECTION ONE – INTRODUCTION

    It's Your Future – Take it Seriously 15

    Where to Turn for Information and Advice 17

    Create an Outline for Your Plan 21

SECTION TWO – STAGE OF LIFE CONSIDERATIONS

    Overview 25

    Early Adult Period 29

    Mid-life Period 37

    Pre-retirement and Retirement Period 43

SECTION THREE – FINANCIAL PLANNING CONSIDERATIONS

    Home Ownership 55

    Building Your Retirement Plan 67

    Monitoring Your Progress 107

    Trends 115

SECTION FOUR – INVESTMENT PLANNING

    Introduction to Investing 123

    Assessing Your Tolerance to Risk 125

    Diversification and Correlation 135

    Asset Classes 145

    Cash 147

        • Fixed Income 151

        • Preferred Shares 159

- Equity 163
- Real Estate Investment Trusts. 171
- Precious metals 175
- Mutual Funds, Segregated Funds & Exchange Traded Funds . 181

Choosing Your Asset Allocation 187

Questionable Investments & Strategies 195

SECTION FIVE – INSURANCE & ESTATE PLANNING

Insurance 215

Estate Planning 225

SECTION SIX – ADMINISTRATION AND PAPERWORK

Choosing an Advisor 235

Establish Your Accounts. 245

Documentation. 255

Fees and Commissions 265

Client Service Agreement 275

Compliance 279

SECTION SEVEN – IMPLEMENTING YOUR PLAN & MANAGING YOUR PORTFOLIO

Implementing Your Plan. 283

Managing Your Portfolio 291

SECTION EIGHT – SUMMARY

Summary 297

Conclusion 305

PREFACE

I HAD ALWAYS BEEN interested in studying the markets and remember looking forward to launching my career in the financial services industry. It was the middle of October 1987 and little did I know that in less than a week after I started, we would experience the biggest stock market crash since Black Monday of 1929.

Since then I have seen the best and the worst of the financial markets. In addition to the market crash in October 1987, I saw the Asian contagion that began in 1997, the tech wreck of 2001 and the credit crisis that led to the financial meltdown of 2008-09. I have seen interest rates drop from over 15% to less than 1% and despite the major corrections that occurred along the way I also experienced the biggest bull market in stock market history.

Today, governments and individual investors around the world are still reeling from the after-effects of the credit crisis. Canadians have felt the impact as well and I have found that my clients are interested in gaining a better understanding of the intricate workings of the financial markets. They want to be better prepared to deal with any unforeseen circumstances that may arise.

These experiences have given me a unique perspective; it is a perspective that I want to share with you.

Despite the popularity of the catchy advertising slogan 'You're richer than you think,' most Canadians will face many financial challenges during their lives. My goal in writing this book was to identify many of the common financial issues you may face throughout your life and provide some guidelines to help you deal with those issues. I also dispel some of the myths surrounding personal finances, expose flawed strategies and outline what you can expect in terms of service.

The book is also a great reference tool. You can keep it handy to look up those hard-to-find facts regarding issues like government benefits, inflation, investment returns, mortgage rates and so on. Inside you will also find links to resources such as financial calculators and other useful financial websites.

It is the kind of book where you should write notes in the margins and bookmark the pages that interest you. The ideas within are meant to be shared and debated with friends, family and colleagues. There will be points of agreement and disagreement but as long as it encourages you to take a closer look at your finances, I will have succeeded in my goals.

There are no inspirational stories of failure turned into success. Instead, you are given the tools to create your own inspirational story and that is the only one that matters.

The research has been done for you and the answers to many of your questions lie within these pages. It comes from scouring such sources as Statistics Canada, Service Canada, the Bank of Canada and many others. Hundreds of hours were spent distilling the data and organizing it into a format that makes the information easy for you to use and understand.

I advocate the use of a financial advisor, who I define as someone who works with you to prepare a financial plan as well as to provide you with the investment advice to help you fulfill that plan. The section on choosing an advisor can be helpful if you are trying to decide whether it is worthwhile or not. As you will see, it involves much more than trying to identify investment opportunities or minimizing fees.

Finally, I wanted to prepare you for the investment experience, including the processes of opening an account with a financial advisor, preparing a financial plan and making investment decisions. I demystify the sometimes vague and complex fee structure that seems to be a characteristic of the investment industry so you can make educated decisions on the products and services you choose.

It is my personal belief that your best insurance when it comes to handling your financial security is to learn the fundamentals. By the time you have finished reading this book you will be well prepared and one step ahead in planning your financial future. Now is the time to begin that journey.

SECTION ONE

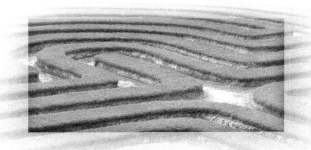

INTRODUCTION

IT'S YOUR FUTURE – TAKE IT SERIOUSLY

MANAGING YOUR PERSONAL finances is a tremendous responsibility; your future depends on it. You need to treat it as a business endeavour and not as something that will take care of itself. Don't count on governments to step in and lend a helping hand either; they are clearly moving in the other direction.

Many look for simple solutions. These can range from the concept of "pay yourself first" to "dollar cost averaging". While they can be components of an overall strategy, these ideas fall far short of being a comprehensive plan. If a plan to manage your finances seems too simple and easy, it probably is.

The risk is that you do not take your finances seriously. For some, it could be because they are disinterested, intimidated, or don't want to face reality. Or it could be because they believe the "system" will care for their needs. Whatever the reason, those who procrastinate or take a casual approach to their personal finances may be faced with unhappy consequences.

Unlike many books that promise easy solutions, I examine many of the challenges you may face in detail. I also provide information and strategies that can help you on the road to success. Treat your money well and it will return the favour.

The result is a book that is more factual than entertaining. Because it is a serious topic, it was a compromise that I was willing to make.

WHERE TO TURN FOR INFORMATION AND ADVICE

Before you begin to tackle the job of managing your personal finances, you need to identify those sources of information that are reliable and as unbiased as possible. A quick review of some of these sources is a good starting point.

Public Media

The primary source of financial information for many Canadians is the public media, including newspapers, magazines, radio and television. They provide us with a virtually unlimited supply of information that needs to be used carefully.

When the media puts information into the hands of the general public it often fails to provide us with guidelines on how we should use it. With the focus on individual investment opportunities and exciting stock picks, the information can be taken out of context. A collection of seemingly good ideas does not necessarily result in a good portfolio. In fact, it may result in a poorly constructed portfolio if the investments do not complement one another.

In their defense, the media are careful to point out that this is information and not advice; however, the public often fails to make the distinction.

Before acting on information from the media you need to determine whether the investment fits your goals, objectives and tolerance to risk. What they cannot see is your personal financial situation or what you are currently holding in your portfolio. Nor do they have to deal with the repercussions of a failed idea.

If you want to proceed with an investment that the media has brought to your attention, you need to ask yourself what it will replace in your portfolio. In other words, what will you sell? If you are adding more cash to your portfolio in order to make the investment, you need to determine how it affects your asset allocation. Will the new mix of investments still be appropriate or will some re-balancing be necessary? Over time adding the latest flavour of the day can cause your portfolio to drift far away from its original form.

There are scores of excellent ideas that appear in the public media. Each may have its own merits on a stand-alone basis but a portfolio of investments must work together. The media has no insight into what you hold and how the addition of an investment they are profiling may affect the performance of your portfolio or, indeed, if the investment itself is appropriate for your situation.

Case studies that appear regularly in our national newspapers are evidence that many people struggle trying to manage finances on their own. The existence of these articles confirms that there is a great leap from theory to reality when you begin to manage your own portfolios.

Self-help books

With all of the self-help books, why are so many people struggling financially?

There is money in selling dreams. Book titles include buzz words like rich, wealthy, profit, secrets and easy. Examples are *The Richest Man in Babylon, Rich Dad Poor Dad, The Wealthy Barber, Smart Couples Finish Rich, Start Late Finish Rich*.

These titles sound more like sales pitches than solutions.

The fact is that the majority of us won't finish rich no matter how many books we read but these titles prey upon our desires to achieve what is almost impossible. Building a comfortable nest egg for retirement won't always be easy; it will be challenging. It will take some sacrifice and it will require your attention to details on an ongoing basis.

Financial advice taken from the do-it-yourself books seems to have the same success as diet books. It works for a while but it is hard to stick to the plan. Eventually, the approach is abandoned for a seemingly easier and more successful approach. It takes more than reading a book to change our behaviour but it doesn't stop us from searching for that easy solution that may be hidden in its pages.

The Internet

The information available on the internet can be overwhelming. The views on the economy, the markets, portfolio construction and individual investments are infinite. The sources of the opinions vary from research reports published by highly reputable firms, to electronic copies of business publications, to independent bloggers whose qualifications are unverified.

Sorting through the maze of information can be an overwhelming task. Whose opinion should you believe; whose advice should you follow?

If the information gleaned from the traditional media should be used carefully, then additional caution should be used when relying on information from obscure internet sites.

Colleagues, friends and relatives

While colleagues, friends and relatives may have the best intentions when passing on investment advice, it should also be used carefully. Their experience tends to be narrow and limited to their own personal situation and their objectives may be completely different from yours.

In conversations among colleagues, there can also be a tendency to talk about investments that have shown strong performance while keeping silent about those that haven't worked out so well. It's human nature; no one wants to broadcast the unfortunate decisions they have made. That can create a perception that the person dispensing the advice is shrewder than they really are.

Be particularly aware of any 'hot tips' that might be passed your way. While you may think your tip is particularly unique, financial advisors have heard hundreds of these stories over the years and a very small percentage of them have ever worked out.

Professional advisors

Financial advisors, financial planners, bankers, insurance agents, real estate agents, accountants and lawyers are all professional advisors. Each has their own particular skill set and is likely to present a situation from the point of view of their profession. Nevertheless, they have the combination of professional training, years of experience and knowledge of your personal situation to help you make the best decisions possible.

In the past, financial advisors were the primary source of information for many investors, but that has changed. With the advent of business channels on television, the internet and smart phones, we are constantly being bombarded with information. One of the new roles of the financial advisor is to act as a filter for that information.

Another role is to remain objective and unemotional about your situation in order to provide the best advice possible. It is a role that will be discussed in more detail later in the book.

Investors often fail to take advantage of the broad range of services available from their financial advisor because they often don't realize what services are offered by the advisor and his firm. Instead, they will often seek the advisor's opinion on an individual investment and nothing else.

After reading this book you will be aware of the broad range of services that may be available and how they may help you manage your personal finances.

Summary

No source of information should be dismissed; the more you read, listen and see, the more you will learn. Over time your experience will help you decide which information is reliable and helpful and which is not. This book should be considered as one of those sources rather than as a source for specific investment advice. It can provide you with some guidance and help you get the most out of the relationship you have with all of your professional advisors. Use it along with some of the other resources I have mentioned and you will be on your way to building a sound financial future.

CREATE AN OUTLINE FOR YOUR PLAN

Even if you have a good idea of how you want to proceed, it can be easy to become overwhelmed by details.

A good approach is to organize your thoughts by building a simple outline of the steps you need to take and then fill in the details later. Whether you are working alone or with an advisor, developing a guide will help to keep you on track. Research shows that writing your ideas down on paper creates a level of personal accountability and increases your chances of success.

You may feel it is either too early in life or too late in life to begin making plans, but nothing could be further from the truth. While your plans will change over time as your life circumstances change, it is important to recognize and address issues that you will face, regardless of your age.

Many want to immediately begin choosing investments without laying the foundation for making their choices. In the absence of a plan, investors risk making poor choices that may be too conservative to meet their needs or too risky for their personal situation.

In this book, we will follow the outline below that you can use as a guide to create an outline for your own personal situation. Throughout the book, we will consider what stage of life you may be at and take that into account. Here are the steps we follow:

- Create a vision for the future. Prioritize your needs and wants for each stage of your life. Ensure that you have balance between your current lifestyle and your future needs.
- Develop a financial plan complete with a retirement budget and projected sources of income, even if you are already retired.
- Assess your personal tolerance to investment risk.
- Develop an investment plan that suits your tolerance to risk. Identify and establish the types of investment accounts that suit your needs.
- Implement your investment plan.
- Monitor your progress against the plan you have drawn up
- Identify any insurance needs that you may have and purchase the appropriate coverage.
- Ensure that you have arranged for estate planning issues, beginning with a will.

Each of these steps is discussed in more detail to provide you with as much information as possible when you are making your financial decisions. As I said before, treat your money well; it is a precious commodity.

Some of the information may seem obvious, some may reveal issues you haven't considered, and some may challenge long-held beliefs.

Section Two

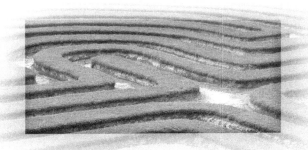

STAGE OF LIFE CONSIDERATIONS

OVERVIEW

The challenges we face will change over the course of our lives. In this section I provide a general overview of the issues that you may face in each stage of life. Later, I delve into the issues in more detail. There is something for everyone. You can read the entire section to develop a feel for my overall philosophy or choose the section or sections that are most relevant to your situation.

The plans you make today and the decisions you make as a result of those plans will shape your life in the future. And a big part of that future will be determined by your financial circumstances.

The planning process begins by creating your vision for the future, making some financial assumptions and calculating whether those goals are achievable. If they are not, adjustments to your plan will need to be made but caution has to be exercised when making those adjustments.

Investors can be tempted to make adjustments to factors they cannot control, such as the rate of return on investments or the rate of inflation. Greater focus should be placed on factors that they can control, such as the amount to spend on a house, the amount to set aside for retirement each month, the age at which to retire and so on.

Once the adjustments have been made, the plan can be recalculated to ensure it is achievable.

A book that everyone should read, regardless of age or financial net worth, is Money Rules by Gail Vaz-Oxlade. It is full of solid advice and the author provides you with simple rules that can help you make sound investment decisions.

Priorities

No matter where you are in your life, it is worthwhile examining what your priorities may be in order to develop an approach that ensures you are successful.

As these priorities change over time, so does the task of managing your finances. While the long term goal of everyone may be to accumulate enough capital for retirement, there are a variety of short term needs that need to be addressed throughout life. The result is a savings program that is not a straight line process.

Regardless of where you are in your life, the key to the successful management of personal financial matters is to keep the various commitments in proper balance. It might look something like this:

Early Adult (20 to 35 years)	**Mid-life** (35 to 55 years)	**Pre-retirement & Retirement** (over 55 years)
Planning	Planning	Planning
Home ownership decisions	Estimating retirement budget	Home ownership decisions
General retirement projections	Estimating savings requirements	Detailed cash flow projections
Risk tolerance analysis	Risk tolerance analysis	Risk tolerance analysis
Investment Strategies	Investment Strategies	Investment Strategies
Mortgage/loan repayments	Elimination of remaining debt	Elimination of remaining debt
Asset accumulation	Asset accumulation	Tax efficient cash flow
Monthly savings plans	Monthly and lump sum savings	RIF withdrawal plans
Growth portfolio	Balanced portfolio	Income portfolio
Accounts	Accounts	Accounts
RRSP contributions	Pension plan contributions	Pension plan withdrawals
TFSA contributions	RRSP contributions	RRIF withdrawals
RESP	TFSA contributions	TFSA withdrawals
Taxable investment accounts	Taxable investment accounts - contributions	Taxable investment accounts – withdrawals
Insurance	Insurance	Insurance
Mortgage insurance	Critical illness insurance	Long term care insurance
Life insurance - income replacement	Reduced life insurance	No life insurance

It is all about knowing your limits and setting guidelines. These guidelines don't have to be hard and fast rules from which you cannot deviate even marginally. Rather, they should serve to provide you with some general direction.

Because everyone has different earning power, different debt levels and different aspirations for both the present and the future, there is no single answer that can be applied.

There are those who don't want to compromise the present to fully fund their retirement portfolios. It is easy to do because the repercussions aren't immediately obvious. However, our government is putting policies in place that will make individuals more responsible for their own retirement, rather than taxing the rest of the population and future generations.

It is worthwhile to examine how some of these priorities may appear at various stage of your life. Each of them will be discussed in more detail.

EARLY ADULT PERIOD

AT THIS STAGE of life, long term retirement plans are probably the last thing on your mind, but it is still a good idea to think about the distant future in broad terms. It is also a period of time when you can accumulate some investment experience and make some mistakes that won't be devastating. Learning from small mistakes can help you to avoid big mistakes later in life.

Planning

While saving for retirement involves building wealth over the long term, everyone has immediate financial commitments and the largest of those is usually the cost of shelter or accommodation. It may be rent or it may involve the purchase of a house along with the associated mortgage payments. For those who have children, a plan to assist with the expenses of a post-secondary education also needs to be considered.

The retirement planning process at this stage may involve simply setting a target date for your retirement and the kind of income you would like to earn in retirement. If your day-to-day expenses have been covered and these additional commitments have been satisfied, any excess income can be used to begin a monthly savings plan.

Financial Situation

A good place to begin is to take stock of your current financial situation by developing a simple household budget and balance sheet. Your **budget represents your cash flow** or income and expenses while your **balance sheet represents your net worth.** It is simply the value of what you own minus any outstanding loans. Both of these items need to be in place before your financial strategy can be developed.

Simplified Household Budget – Sample Only		
Budget Item	**Income**	**Expenses**
Total Income	$50,000	
Income tax		$10,000
CPP & EI contributions		$3250
Food & Drink (including restaurant dining)		$7500
Clothing		$1750
Transportation		$3500
Healthcare		$2000
Entertainment & recreation		$2000
Personal care		$750
Miscellaneous		$1500
Retirement Savings		$2000
Housing (mortgage or rent plus utilities and taxes)		$14000
Vacation & Travel		$1750
Total	$50,000	$50,000

Simplified Household Balance Sheet – Sample Only			
Assets	Value (Assets)	Loans (Liabilities)	Net Worth
Home	$350,000	$175,000	$175,000
Other real estate	0	0	0
Vehicles	$26,000	$9,500	$16,500
Other personal assets	$10,000	0	$10,000
Bank Accounts	$2,000	0	$2,000
Investment accounts, TFSAs and RRSPs	$21,000	0	$21,000
Pension plan assets	0	0	0
Home equity line of credit	0	$8,000	-$8,000
Credit card balance	0	$1,700	-$1,700
Other debt	0	0	0
Totals	$409,000	$194,200	$214,800

Accommodation Expenses

Whether you choose to rent or to buy a home, the cost of accommodation requires a major financial commitment. Your choices in this area will affect the amount you will have available for investment. As a result, this topic needs careful consideration and is discussed in more detail later.

Education Funding

Over four years the tuition costs at a Canadian university can easily be over $25,000 in today's dollars and books can add another $1,000 to $1,500 per year. Those figures don't cover expenses related to accommodation, food, transportation, clothing or spending money.

Registered Educational Saving Plans (RESPs) are an important tool when you are planning how much you want to set aside for future education expenses.

Even if the cost of a child's education cannot be completely covered, taking advantage of government grants by establishing an RESP account is a sound strategy. Each dollar in government grants is a dollar that you do not have to earn or borrow. In addition, any growth on your investments within an RESP is tax-free growth.

Every family will be different but taking advantage of the maximum grant by contributing $2500 per year to an RESP is a good start. If you can't afford $2500, try to contribute what you can. The government grant that equals 20% of your annual contribution is free money.

Post-secondary education does not have to be a free ride for your children. Students can help by working summer jobs and taking student loans. Their contribution can help to develop an appreciation for their education and it can provide a sense of accomplishment. But minimizing the liabilities they will face upon graduation will help them to establish themselves financially early in life.

Investment Strategies

In the beginning your investment program will probably be modest.

The major expense you may be facing at this stage of life is your accommodation expense. There is always the choice between renting and buying but the choice is not as straightforward as many would make it appear. For the first twenty years or more of your working life, mortgage payments may inhibit your ability to set aside significant savings.

A second major expense, as mentioned, can be funding post-secondary education for your children. The government provides incentives to help you achieve that objective.

Your first investment portfolio

Opening an account and beginning an investment program early, even if it is modest, provides significant benefits. This account can be a taxable investment account, a tax-free savings account or an RRSP account.

The *first benefit* is the knowledge you gain about the investment process and the financial markets. What you learn about yourself and how you react to financial situations that arise can be just as important as learning how to identify investment opportunities.

Investors tend to learn much more quickly when their own money is at stake because one of the key elements involved in the decision making process is learning what their emotional reaction will be when their investments begin to gain or lose value. You can practice your investing skills by making hypothetical investments, but because you aren't playing with real money it is easy to be calm and objective. That changes when your own money is at stake.

Determining your ability to deal with the ups and downs of the investment markets will define what kind of an investor you will become. It is easier to learn that earlier in life.

The *second benefit* is that you are actually building wealth even if it is at a modest pace. One of the keys to wealth creation that is often overlooked is maintaining the discipline to contribute regularly to your portfolio. Beginning early and developing good financial management habits will serve you well down the road.

The tables below illustrate the growth of investments and the difference between earning a low return on your investments and earning a modest return on your investments.

	Growth investments at 3.0% annual rate of return					
	Value after					
Monthly deposit	5 years	10 years	15 years	20 years	25 years	30 years
$100	$6,562	$14,169	$22,988	$26,897	$45,063	$58,803
$500	$32,810	$70,845	$114,940	$134,485	$225,315	$294,015
$1000	$65,620	$141,690	$229,880	$268,970	$450,630	$588,030

Growth investments at 5.0% annual rate of return						
	Value after					
Monthly deposit	5 years	10 years	15 years	20 years	25 years	30 years
$100	$6,962	$15,848	$27,188	$41,663	$60,136	$83,712
$500	$34,810	$79,240	$135,940	$208,315	$300,680	$418,560
$1000	$69,620	$158,480	$271,880	$416,630	$601,360	$837,120

Mutual funds are a good choice to begin with in your investment program because they can be purchased in relatively small amounts. As time goes on, experience is gained and more money becomes available for investment; you can then look to add other elements to your portfolio. It might be exchange traded funds (ETFs), an individual stock, a corporate bond or one of countless other investments available to you.

Accounts

The question of priorities often arises. Should excess income be dedicated to paying down an existing mortgage or should a savings plan be started?

At this stage of life, making additional mortgage payments is an excellent investment. You will be debt-free earlier in life which will give you the flexibility to begin a more significant savings plan at that time. Additionally, being debt-free can provide peace of mind in the event of illness, unemployment or any other unforeseen difficulty that may arise.

If you have already committed to making extra mortgage payments and still have excess funds available for investment, you can open an RRSP account, a Tax Free Savings Account (TFSA), an investment account or all three. If you have children, consider opening a Registered Educational Savings Plan (RESP).

Insurance

Your working life often begins by assuming large financial and personal commitments. Debt may be high while assets are modest. Marriage, your first home and children may be introduced into your life. These are long term responsibilities and they need to be taken care of in the event of your absence.

Life insurance is protection against the loss of income in the event that the insured person dies. Those who survive you and *who depend on that income* benefit from the insurance policy. This is an important definition.

You do not need life insurance if you are single with no dependents, even if you have a mortgage. You also do not need life insurance policies on your children because they have no income. You would suffer a severe emotional hardship but not a financial one.

Calculate the appropriate amount of life insurance for your situation and buy term life insurance.

Notes:

- Your household budget represents your income and your expenses
- Your household balance sheet represents your assets (what you own) and your liabilities (your debt obligations).
- The government will provide matching grants of up to $500 per year for Registered Educational Saving Plans

MID-LIFE PERIOD

AT THIS STAGE of life a great many expenses will be coming to an end or may have already disappeared if you haven't burdened yourself with unnecessary debt during the earlier stages of your working career. If that is not likely to happen, you need to go back to your household budget and balance sheet and modify your financial strategies. Once these financial obligations have been addressed, your free cash flow will be significantly higher than during your early working years.

Planning

Planning for your retirement now takes on an increased importance, yet many Canadians in this group still fall into the trap of taking their retirement for granted. Some never give it a passing thought, some want to live for today and let the future take care of itself and some simply believe that the government will take care of them. All of these mindsets are dangerous to your financial health and your lifestyle in retirement.

A survey conducted by Leger Marketing for CIBC in July 2012 found that fewer than half of Canadians between the ages of 50 and 59 had less than $100,000 saved for retirement. The same survey found that 53% of Canadians planned to continue working after retirement. One-third of those who anticipated working in retirement would do so for the money.

At some point the light does go on for everyone. For some it is too late. They are already in retirement and realize there will be a shortfall. It is a painful experience to realize that the next twenty-five years of your life could be at a standard of living far below expectations.

The earlier the light goes on, the more likely that the goal of a comfortable retirement will be achieved. Review your household budget and your net worth. These documents provide a reference point for the state of your current financial situation and the progress that you are making.

It is during this time of your life that serious savings for retirement can and need to begin. There is not a magical age at which this happens because the other major commitments for each of us disappear at different times. It is an argument for tackling those commitments early to allow the retirement savings to begin as soon as possible.

While it may be extremely difficult for someone who is thirty-five years old to justify saving for a retirement that is thirty years in the future, they will look back happily at their decision to plan early. A review of your current financial situation can bring that into focus.

If you have significant debt or are adding to your debt burden at this stage of life, you need to re-evaluate your financial situation. Develop a comprehensive plan to get yourself back on track as soon as possible. If you don't know where to begin, find a financial advisor who can help you with your situation.

Now is the time to prepare more detailed financial projections. Visualize your retirement lifestyle and estimate what kind of income you will need to fund that lifestyle. From there you can determine with some degree of accuracy how much capital you will need to accumulate and with that information you can calculate how much you will need to set aside on a monthly or annual basis.

Investment Strategies

Any excess cash flow can be directed toward building your investment portfolio. You may have begun an investment program earlier in life even if you did not have any defined goals in mind. With the benefit of a plan, those objectives become more clearly defined and it becomes an easy step to accelerate your investment program.

A common approach

In the beginning many investment plans start with an RRSP contribution. For many, it is simply a way to reduce the amount of income tax we pay each year with no long term goals in mind. Everyone likes a refund at tax time and the deductions we are able to claim for our contributions are a strong incentive. Although that approach is better than not making a contribution, it is an aimless strategy.

While the deductions may be an incentive, the real reason we should be making these contributions is to accumulate enough savings to help fund a comfortable retirement.

As it is, most people contribute far less than what they are allowed. In 2008 the median contribution was about $2700 (http://www42.statcan.gc.ca/smr08/2011/smr08_154_2011-eng.htm), far less than the average contribution limit. It is clear that despite incentives, Canadians are not maximizing their RRSPs. Maybe they don't need to, but without a plan, how can they be sure?

Clearly, by providing us with incentives to invest for the long term, our government wants us to take on more responsibility for financial independence in retirement. The fact that they have introduced tax-free savings accounts (TFSAs) to supplement RRSP accounts as a means to save for retirement underscores that view. So do the impending changes to the Canada Pension Plan and Old Age Security.

If you have not already done so, establish some long term objectives and begin a serious plan for saving for retirement. Your contributions to your program can be monthly, on a lump sum basis or a combination of both. The goal is to accumulate capital for your retirement and to monitor that progress.

Accounts

You will probably be in a higher tax bracket than you were earlier in life and maximizing RRSP contributions should be a priority. Your TFSA should also be a priority. If you haven't already done so, you can make up for contributions missed in previous years.

There are those who are fortunate enough to have sufficient assets and disposable income to fund a taxable investment account in addition to their RRSP account and their TFSA. If you are in that group, examine the impact of taxes on your investment decisions.

For those without pension plans, a general rule of thumb when saving for retirement is to maximize your RRSP contributions first, followed by contributions to your TFSA, and only then should you begin to contribute to a taxable investment account.

Insurance

Your life insurance needs should be reduced at this point. If your mortgage is not paid, the amount owing should be far less than it was and you should no longer need to be funding educational savings plans. These reduced commitments, along with your ability to generate income from investments, offset the need to maintain a policy that provided the same benefits as required earlier in life.

One form of insurance worth examining is critical illness insurance. It differs from life insurance in that it provides you with a benefit while you are still alive. If you contract a critical illness covered by this type of policy, you may be eligible for a lump sum cash benefit to be used for whatever purpose you desire.

Mid-life Period

NOTES:

- A Notice of Assessment is issued by the Canada Revenue Agency after you have submitted your tax return. It usually arrives in May or June and will tell you what your RRSP contribution limit will be. You have until the end of February the following year to make that contribution for the current tax year.

- Contribution limits are up to 18% of earned income but the average Canadian contributes less than $3000 per year.

- The need for life insurance may be reduced at this point in your life.

PRE-RETIREMENT AND RETIREMENT PERIOD

I F YOU ARE already retired, the opportunity to add to your investment portfolio has probably passed and you are left to work with what you have. It is critical that you have eliminated all debt including mortgage debt and other consumer debt. Servicing debt from an investment portfolio makes no financial sense.

Those who were disciplined and made the necessary sacrifices during the early and middle years of their lives should be well positioned. Those who didn't may face struggles and could have some hard, unpleasant choices to make.

Planning

In your retirement years your focus on planning should shift to maintaining a suitable level of income. Some of this income may come from sources such as CPP, OAS and employer pension plans but if you are like most people, that income will need to be supplemented from your own personal investments.

In Canada, the sources of retirement income during the period from 2000 to 2002 are shown in the following tables. This data illustrates the relatively low reliance on income from RRSP investments but even more surprising may be the amount of income seniors derived from employment. For some, employment may be by choice, while for others it may be necessity. Regardless of what your situation might be, it is an important source of income to keep in mind.

Sources of Income for Seniors (3 year average 2000-2002)		
Source of Income	**Ages 65 to 74**	**Age 75 and over**
Employment	14.0%	3.3%
Old Age Security	19.3%	24.1%
Canada Pension Plan	17.5%	18.1%
Employer Pensions	28.2%	28.6%
Investment (non-RRSP)	12.1%	18.6%
RRSP	2.7%	2.4%
Note: Does not sum to 100 because minor income sources are excluded.		
Source: Statcan		

As Canadians we are fortunate to have programs like Old Age Security and the Canada Pension Plan to help fund our retirements to provide a very basic level of income. However, you will need to supplement that with income from your personal savings and your employer pension plan (if you have one) in order to generate enough income for a comfortable lifestyle.

You also need to examine the savings you have accumulated during your working years. It is these savings from which you will be deriving retirement income. If you exceeded your goals, you can probably draw a larger income than you had planned for; if you fell short of your goals, you will have to develop a strategy to address your shortfalls.

If you are very near to retirement or already in retirement, what you have accumulated in your savings and pension plans will be what you have to work with. The ability to add significantly to either will have passed.

Your planning at this stage of life should revolve around developing detailed cash flow projections. You need to know the sources of your income and the amount you can expect from each source. There can be varying levels of Old Age Security (OAS) and Canada Pension Plan (CPP) payments. You may have income from an employer pension and you may have personal accounts such as a RRIF, a TFSA and a taxable investment account.

Prior to retirement, your employment or business generated the income required to cover living expenses and the extra that you set aside in the form of savings. All of that changes with retirement. There is no employment income to fall back on and there may be very little in the way of excess capital should things not work out as planned. In that situation it becomes even more critical to make the appropriate investment choices, and developing your investment profile through a risk tolerance analysis can be invaluable.

Withdrawal Strategies

The importance of selecting a ***realistic withdrawal rate*** to generate income in your retirement cannot be overestimated. Reaching for higher investment returns and basing your withdrawals on that higher estimated return can increase volatility, which in turn increases the probability of portfolio failure.

Even the most conservative portfolio will not have a consistent return over the course of many years. There will be some variance in the rate of return and an appropriate withdrawal may require a compromise between income requirements and preserving the integrity of your portfolio.

Rather than choose ***a fixed amount*** from a portfolio each year, choose ***a percentage*** of the value of your portfolio.

RIF Withdrawal Strategy

The Canada Revenue Agency (CRA) already provides useful guidelines in the form of their minimum withdrawal requirements. It uses a percentage of account value to determine withdrawals as outlined in the following table. You can follow these guidelines or develop your own customized withdrawal strategy.

Using these CRA withdrawal requirements, at the end of each year multiply the year-end value of the account from which you are withdrawing income by the withdrawal factor (percentage). That will determine your income from that account for the subsequent twelve months.

Minimum RRIF Withdrawals as a Percentage of the Value of Your RRIF (as of 2012)									
Age	Withdrawal Factor	Age	Withdrawal Factor	Age	Withdrawal Factor	Age	Withdrawal Factor	Age	Withdrawal Factor
60	3.33%	65	4.00%	70	5.00%	75	7.85%	80	8.75%	85	10.33%
61	3.45%	66	4.17%	71	7.38%	76	7.99%	81	8.99%	86	10.79%
62	3.57%	67	4.35%	72	7.48%	77	8.15%	82	9.27%	87	11.33%
63	3.70%	68	4.55%	73	7.59%	78	8.33%	83	9.58%	88	11.96%
64	3.85%	69	4.76%	74	7.71%	79	8.53%	84	9.93%	89	12.71%

An example of a customized withdrawal strategy

When trying to determine a reasonable and sustainable level of withdrawal from your investments each year, the minimum RRIF withdrawal guidelines are a good place to start, or you can develop a customized withdrawal strategy.

The following example uses two simple calculations that provide a reasonable guideline:

- *Step One* – *subtract your age* in the year of withdrawal from age 90. At age 60, for example, the difference would be 30.

- *Step Two* – *divide the value* of your investments at the beginning of the year by the number calculated in step one. The answer will provide you with the level of withdrawal for the upcoming year.

Repeat the calculation at the beginning of each year to determine your level of withdrawal for the upcoming year.

Portfolio Withdrawal Estimator											
Age	Factor	Age	Factor	Age	Factor	Age	Factor	Age	Factor	Age	Factor
60	30	65	25	70	20	75	15	80	10	85	5
61	29	66	24	71	19	76	14	81	9	86	4
62	28	67	23	72	18	77	13	82	8	87	3
63	27	68	22	73	17	78	12	83	7	88	2
64	26	69	21	74	16	79	11	84	6	89	1

Using this table to provide an estimate, a 70 year old investor with a $500,000 investment portfolio can withdraw $25,000 ($500,000 divided by 20 = $25,000).

There are online calculators available that can provide customized calculations using various life expectancy estimates. One example can be seen at www.moneypages.ca.

Addressing Shortfalls

If you have a shortfall between your income requirements and your actual retirement income, then more drastic action may have to be taken in order to ensure that your income will be sustainable throughout your life. It can range from reducing your spending to downsizing your house or engaging in part-time employment if you are still able to do so. Another option is to postpone retirement for a year or two. There are no easy answers but it is better to make the decisions when you still have some control over the situation.

There can be resistance to those strategies because of human nature. Do others consider you a failure, or do you consider yourself a failure, if these are the options you choose? Does your social status decline? What will your friends think? Will they avoid you? The answer is probably "no" to most of these questions. It is amazing how much pressure these thoughts have on you and it may delay making a sound decision. It can become image over substance.

If you develop a sound retirement strategy you can make those decisions when they are right for you rather than when they are forced upon you.

Everyone needs to be realistic and everyone's reality is different. If you can't keep up with the Joneses, don't try. Set your own standards for a lifestyle... one that you can afford without worry.

Investment Strategies

You need to examine all of your investment strategies to ensure the ongoing sustainability of your retirement income. The focus should shift from generating growth to generating consistent income.

The importance of earning a reasonable rate of return generated by your portfolio is obvious but an often over-looked concern is the effect of volatility on a portfolio from which income is being drawn. Just as volatility can be helpful when building a portfolio with a dollar cost averaging strategy, withdrawing funds from a volatile portfolio can have a disastrous effect.

Your portfolio should be analyzed to ensure that it has an appropriate balance between rate of return potential and volatility characteristics. Considering only rate of return in the absence of volatility misses an important part of the picture. Considering only the safety of principal without protection against the rising cost of living overlooks another important issue.

Accounts

Your taxable investment accounts and your TFSA can remain intact upon retirement; however, you may want to change the overall makeup of these accounts somewhat to reflect your need for income over growth.

RRSP options at retirement

When you want begin to withdrawing income from assets accumulated in your RRSP account, you have three basic options. Whatever option you choose, you must make a choice by the end of the year in which you turn 71. You can make the decision earlier but Canada Revenue Agency regulations mandate that you make your choice no later than age 71.

- You can collapse the RRSP and withdraw all of the cash, minus taxes owing which will be substantial. This is the least attractive option.
- A second option is to use the proceeds from your RRSP to purchase an annuity.
- The third option is to convert your RRSP to a Registered Retirement Income Fund (RRIF).

Pension Plan options at retirement

Should you have a *defined benefit pension plan,* it should remain in place. It will provide you with a guaranteed income for life regardless of how long you live. These plans are becoming less common because of the high and uncertain cost to the employer.

Defined contribution pension plans are another story. Upon retirement they are treated in a similar manner to an RRSP and as an investor you have a decision to make. You can choose an annuity or you can move them into an account that is similar to a RRIF. Depending upon the jurisdiction it may be a Life Income Fund (LIF), a Locked-in Retirement Income Fund (LRIF) or a Prescribed Retirement Income Fund (PRIF).

Annuities are a life insurance product and while they have some advantages, they are very *inflexible.* If a circumstance arises where you need additional income in a given year, you will not be able to increase your annuity income.

Retirement income funds are much more flexible but they lack the guarantees provided by an annuity. Each has their own unique features and it is a good idea to discuss these features with your financial advisor in order to have a better understanding of any account limitations.

Portfolio volatility and the effect on income

Volatility is the enemy of an income oriented portfolio.

Without describing the process in detail, a **Monte Carlo** simulation tool can compare the results of various portfolios by combining their rate of return and volatility characteristics. Results of Monte Carlo simulations illustrate a direct relationship between the volatility of a portfolio and its ability to survive over a long period of withdrawals.

These simulations clearly show that portfolios with increased volatility have an increased chance of failure over less volatile portfolios that generate an equivalent rate of return.

Even a sophisticated calculator cannot predict a safe withdrawal rate with absolute precision because a safe withdrawal rate depends on two factors: rate of return AND volatility. In order to minimize the detrimental effect of volatility on your portfolio, every effort should be made to minimize volatility and, in conjunction with that, a sound withdrawal strategy needs to be developed.

A *simple hypothetical comparison* between two portfolios can illustrate the effect of volatility. Using the same two portfolios as in the previous illustration, you can see that withdrawals from a volatile portfolio can exacerbate the situation. The difference in value of the two portfolios *after only three years* is almost $6,000. Over the entire period of your retirement the effect of volatility would be even more dramatic.

	Low volatility portfolio				High volatility portfolio			
	Beginning Value	Rate of Return	Withdrawal	Ending Value	Beginning Value	Rate of Return	Withdrawal	Ending Value
Year One	$100,000	-5%	$10,000	$85,000	$100,000	-20%	$10,000	$70,000
Year Two	$85,000	5%	$10,000	$79,250	$70,000	20%	$10,000	$74,000
Year Three	$79,250	12%	$10,000	$78,760	$74,000	12%	$10,000	$72,880

Insurance

In many cases life insurance will not be necessary at this point in your life. Your retirement funds should be in place and in the event of your death any assets in your RRIF can roll over tax-free to your spouse. You can also name your spouse as the beneficiary of your TFSA and even if you don't, there are no tax consequences associated with collapsing that account. Your taxable investment accounts can be held in joint names and can continue to generate income for the surviving spouse.

If you don't have a spouse upon your retirement or if your spouse predeceases you in retirement, your RRSP will be collapsed upon your death and taxes will be due. At that point it doesn't matter. Remember the definition of insurance:

> *Life insurance is protection against the loss of income in the event that the insured person dies. Those who survive you, and who depend on that income, benefit from the insurance policy.*

Since you are either unmarried or have no surviving spouse, there should be no one dependent on the income from your RRIF.

Long term care insurance may be more applicable for those who are recently retired. However, premiums have risen in recent years even for existing policy holders. The cost of coverage can be expensive, especially for those who purchase that coverage later in life, and several insurance carriers have chosen to discontinue long term care insurance in 2012.

Transition to Retirement

The transition to retirement is a step into the unknown. Not only does your employment income come to an end, the entire structure of your day changes. Your social network may change dramatically since you will no longer have co-workers. Your sense of accomplishment may also change in retirement.

Being well-prepared emotionally, socially and financially is the key to an enjoyable retirement.

Notes:

- Volatility of returns is an important consideration if you are retired.
- Cost of living increases must also be considered.
- A sound strategy for withdrawing income from your investment portfolio is imperative.
- Develop a plan to deal with any shortfalls between your income requirements in retirement and your actual income in retirement.

SECTION THREE

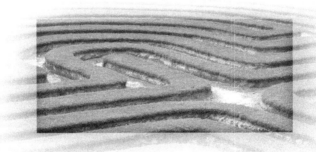

FINANCIAL PLANNING CONSIDERATIONS

HOME OWNERSHIP

Home ownership usually occupies a significant position in both the budget and the balance sheet. Since it is one of the largest financial commitments you can make in your life, the issue of home ownership needs to be discussed objectively. Resist the temptation to include any anticipated increase in the value of your home as a source of funds for retirement.

Two questions arise. Is it better to rent or own? If I decide on ownership, what is a reasonable amount to spend? The answers are less obvious than they may seem.

Rent vs. Own

An important consideration is whether or not home ownership makes financial sense for your current situation or whether renting is the better option. The answer to this question is far from obvious and often influenced by many misconceptions that have become ingrained in our psyche.

You may ask, "What about throwing money away on rent and not building any home equity?" The counter to that argument is, "What about throwing your money away on interest?" For many people who buy a home, the major cost is not the house; it is the interest they pay on the mortgage.

That money doesn't go to building equity; it goes directly to the bank and it can be more than the value of the house itself.

In order to make an accurate comparison, you need to take into account the mortgage payments, taxes, utility costs, maintenance and condo fees (if any) when comparing the cost of a house to apartment rental. For older homes, the cost of renovations and upgrades is often a cost that is overlooked. You should also consider how much you could have made if you had invested the down payment rather than used it for the purposes of buying a house.

The cost of renting an apartment typically consists of your rent and some utilities. If that number is less than the cost of home ownership, **the difference can be invested for growth**. That is how you build equity when you are renting.

It is a difficult comparison to make because so many factors need to be considered. Without considering the investment aspect, these considerations include:

- *Price:* Is the house market over or undervalued with respect to rental prices? This is not a straight forward comparison because of the many factors that need to be considered.

- *Stability of payments:* Those who are concerned with the possibility of rental price increases over time may like the security of knowing that their mortgage payment is fixed, thus providing some certainty for budgeting purposes. However, mortgage rates are constantly changing and the possibility of a significant rise in mortgage rates can put a family budget in jeopardy. Taxes and condo fees are also subject to change (increase) with little control for the owner. So, while the notion of having a stable payment for budgetary purposes is nice in theory, in practice the home owner faces as many obstacles to price stability as does the renter.

- *Pride of ownership:* This is an aspect that is very difficult to quantify, but it cannot be dismissed out of hand. It is important to differentiate between the pride of ownership (a house that you can actually afford) and satisfying the desire to live in a big house with a mortgage that can create severe economic hardship if interest rates rise.

- *Ability to personalize your home*: If a homeowner wants to build a deck, fence or renovate a bathroom he just has to do it. As a renter, you may have less luck in getting a landlord to change a bathtub just because you don't like the color. However, even property owners are subject to limitations. This is particularly true in the case of condos or townhomes.

- *Duration of ownership*: Transaction fees for real estate purchases and sales can be significant. If the expected duration of your stay is relatively short, the transaction fees can put you in the red, even if the value of the home has increased. Some of these fees are: real estate agent fees, legal fees, land transfer taxes, CMHC mortgage insurance, mortgage closing costs and so on. The idea of a young couple buying a "starter home" with the intention of moving up in 3 or 4 years once they have "built equity", makes a lot of sense to a realtor who is collecting commissions, but very little sense to a family who might see all their "equity" end up in the hands of third parties.

A useful calculator that takes these factors and others into consideration can be seen at: www.moneypages.ca.

Renting until the purchase of a home makes financial sense is a strategy worth considering; just remember to invest the difference to build your wealth. It is unlikely that your banker or real estate agent will promote that strategy because it is not in their best interests, but it may be in yours.

For a great many people, the **image of home ownership** is a bigger factor in their decision than the financial reality. It can be an easy leap to convince yourself that bigger is better when it is something that you want but don't really need.

Dangerous debt levels

Home ownership has been used as a status symbol in recent years but few people realize the cost of that status symbol. The following chart illustrates the growth in debt that Canadians have assumed when compared to their income levels; a level of debt that may be unsustainable.

The only reason that they can still afford to make the payments on these debts is because interest rates have remained at historically low levels in recent years. Should those rates rise even marginally, a great many Canadians could be at risk of defaulting on their payments.

None of this is an indictment of home ownership, but if it is the path you choose, **choose what you need and what is affordable** rather than what you want. You should have a good idea of what that is before you talk to your banker or your real estate agent.

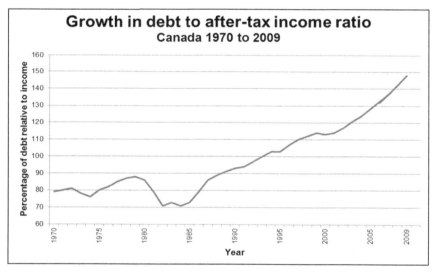

Source: Statistics Canada, CANSIM tables 380-0019 and 378-0051
http://www.statcan.gc.ca/pub/11-008-x/2011001/c-g/11430/desc/desc002-eng.htm

What is affordable?

For those who want to own a home, they should **buy one that they can afford**. If it happens that you can afford an expensive home, there is nothing wrong with that. However, the balance sheet of many Canadians indicates that far too much emphasis is being placed on real estate without regard to overall finances.

The question isn't just whether you can afford a home at today's mortgage rates; it is whether you can afford the home in a "normal" interest rate environment.

A study by the Bank of Canada found that:

> *"While measures of housing affordability remain favourable, this is largely because interest rates are unusually low. Rates will not remain at their current levels forever. The impact of eventual increases is likely to be greater than in previous cycles, given the higher stock of debt owed by Canadian households. At a 4 per cent **real mortgage interest rate**—equivalent to the average rate since 1995—affordability falls to its worst level in 16 years."*

When the Bank of Canada talks about a real mortgage interest rate of 4%, it is referring to the amount by which mortgage rates exceed inflation. In other words, if inflation rates averaged 2%, then mortgage rates would have averaged about 6%.

When determining what you can afford, some lenders will base that affordability on the lowest mortgage rate available, but that is a strategy that leaves no margin for error. Interest rates will fluctuate and anyone who lived through the mortgage rates of the early 1980s can tell you horror stories.

As the Governor of the Bank of Canada, Mark Carney, said in his address to the Vancouver Board of Trade in 2011, "**Even a fixed rate mortgage will re-price a number of times over the life of a mortgage**".

The following chart illustrates the 5 year rate on mortgages over the past fifty years. The average rate over that time has been in excess of 9% with rates peaking at over 18% in 1982. Many homeowners who have been counting on interest rates to stay low forever could face financial hardship should rates approach historical averages.

Monthly payments on a $250,000 mortgage with a 25 year amortization would go from $1285 with a 3.75% interest rate to $2100 with a 9% rate. Payments would increase by over $800 per month!

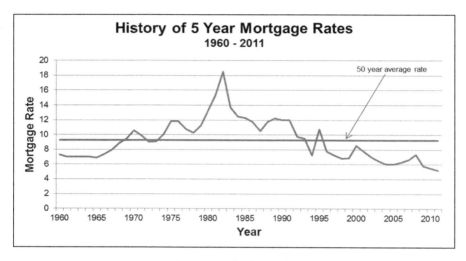

Source: Bank of Canada

INTEREST RATES AND AFFORDABILITY

When calculating affordability, use the higher of the current mortgage rates or a rate that is approximately 4% over inflation. The inflation rate in Canada over the past 25 years has averaged between 2.25% and 2.5%. That means you should use a hypothetical interest rate of at least 6.25% and 6.5% when calculating affordability.

Let's assume that your calculations indicate that you could afford a mortgage payment of approximately $1700 per month. That would equate to a mortgage of $250,000 at 6.5% for 25 years. In this case, you would set your limit for a mortgage at $250,000 and then begin shopping for rates. If you could find a rate for 3.75%, your payments would only be about $1285 per month.

By spending less than you can afford, you would have a cushion of $415 per month in the event that interest rates rise. One strategy would be to apply that $415 per month directly towards the principal of your mortgage. If rates remained constant, you would have paid your mortgage off six years early and if rates rose, your home would still be affordable.

The question isn't necessarily whether you can afford to make your mortgage payments at current rates; it is whether you can afford the payments when rates are near their historical norms, which is about 4% above the inflation rate.

In the first decade of the 2000s we have been living outside of a normal interest rate environment where rates have been equal to, or lower than, inflation. It has lulled many into the impression that these are normal circumstances, but they are not. Historically, five year mortgage rates have averaged about 4% over inflation. In 2012 these rates were close to 1% or 2% above inflation.

In a 2012 poll conducted by Harris Decima, 29% of Canadians felt a rise of two points in interest rates would make it difficult for them to meet their mortgage payments and a further 29% would be severely affected by a rise of three or four points in interest rates. Don't count on mortgage rates staying low forever; build in a cushion.

The following table compares two couples who are trying to determine what they can afford in terms of a house purchase. The first couple has determined that they can get a mortgage for 3.75% and have based their affordability on that rate. They are counting on rates remaining at the current level or falling for the duration of their mortgage. The second couple also realizes they can get a mortgage for 3.75% but want to be sure that they can still afford the house if rates rise to 6.5%.

In the end, they both take out a mortgage for 3.75% but the second couple has purchased a more affordable house with a smaller mortgage. If rates did climb, this couple could still afford the payments.

As we have seen, mortgage rates over the past fifty years have been above 3.75% for a much longer period of time than they have been below that level. Be realistic when calculating what you can afford.

Other home ownership costs

There are additional costs to maintaining your home that need to be considered. These will include property taxes, utilities, insurance and maintenance. The actual cost of many of these items can be obtained from your real estate agent or from the person who is selling the home. A rough guide for estimating the annual property taxes is about 1.0% to 1.25% of the property value. An estimate on utilities and insurance is also necessary to determine your total monthly expenses and ultimately the size of a mortgage you can safely afford.

The value of a house you can afford depends on a combination of the down payment and the affordability of the total monthly payments that you might be faced with. The total cost of your mortgage, property taxes, insurance, utilities and any condo fees should represent no more than 30% of your gross income. That will leave room for other budget expenses.

Don't forget to factor in the transaction costs that are associated with the purchase of a home. Typically, real estate fees are absorbed by the seller, but as a purchaser you will still be faced with closing costs which include, among other things, legal fees.

Affordability Calculations		
	3.75% interest	**6.5% interest**
Annual Income	$90,000	$90,000
Total payments for housing as a percent of income	30%	30%
Total acceptable payments for housing	$27,000 per year	$27,000 per year
Total acceptable payments per month	$2250	$2250
- Property taxes (monthly)	$275	$250
- All utilities & insurance (monthly)	$325	$325
- Available for mortgage (monthly)	$1650	$1675
Amortization period	25 years	25 years
Total affordable mortgage	At 3.75% = $322,000	At 6.5% = $248,000

Extra caution should be used when buying an older home. Significant repair, maintenance and renovation expenses can add to the cost. A home inspection is advised, and if any issues are identified, the cost of addressing those issues must be incorporated into the cost of your home.

Canada Mortgage and Housing Corporation (CMHC)

When considering the purchase of a home, most lenders will require a minimum down payment of 5% of the purchase price. With a down payment of 5% you will be faced with paying high CMHC fees which adds to the overall transaction costs. The fee declines as the down payment increases and with a down payment of 20% or more. Because of the additional costs of CMHC fees, a down payment of more than 5% is desirable, while 20% or more is preferable.

Other obligations

Before making the decision to purchase a house, other factors come into play. You may have a car loan or lease, a student loan, a line of credit or other payment obligations. All of these obligations, along with your mortgage payment, represent your total debt service costs. The amount of these obligations divided by your total gross income represents your total debt service ratio.

According to Investopedia, the debt service ratio is a

> *"measure that financial lenders use as a rule of thumb to give a preliminary assessment of whether a potential borrower is already in too much debt. More specifically, this ratio shows the proportion of gross income that is already spent on housing-related and other similar payments. Receiving a ratio of less than 40% means that the potential borrower has an acceptable level of debt."*
>
> Read more: http://www.investopedia.com/terms/t/totaldebtserviceratio.asp#ixzz29Ubwq362

In other words, the decision to purchase a home cannot be made without considering your other financial obligations. Choices may have to be made. Some of these may be a smaller home, a less expensive car or deferring a purchase until your financial situation warrants taking out a mortgage and making a major purchase.

Keep in mind that **the job of the banker** is to lend you as much money as you can afford with minimal risk of default. Their job is not to set you up with a mortgage that represents a reasonable level of payments and that leaves you with enough to enjoy a comfortable lifestyle and the ability to save for retirement.

If you buy a home you can afford there **may be an opportunity to upgrade** if and when your financial situation dictates that the added expenses will fit within your new budget. Be sure to factor in real estate fees, closing costs on the sale of your existing home and closing costs on the purchase of your new home if you are thinking of making a change.

The truth is that the less you spend on real estate, the more you will have for lifestyle expenses and the more you can set aside for assets that can generate long term growth for your retirement. And if you can't afford to upgrade, at least you have not put yourself at a financial disadvantage by taking on more debt than you can afford.

An easy-to-use affordability calculator can be found on Rate Hub's website at: http://www.ratehub.ca/mortgage-affordability-calculator. Their site also provides a convenient way for potential homebuyers to compare mortgage rates.

Additional payments against the principal owing on your mortgage can be considered as savings, rather than the cost of shelter. It not only saves significant interest costs, it also allows your mortgage to be repaid more quickly. Once your mortgage is repaid, a greater percentage of your income can be re-directed to building your investment portfolio.

Some advisors do not advocate paying down a mortgage. It may be because they truly believe it is a poor strategy or it may be because they would like the additional funds flowing into the accounts they manage. Don't hesitate to ask lots of questions about the advantages and disadvantages of paying down your mortgage.

NOTES:

- In the long term, mortgage rates have averaged about 4% above inflation.
- When calculating the affordability of a home, the total monthly costs involved in owning that home should not exceed 30% of gross household income.
- The total of all monthly mortgage and load payments should not exceed 40% of your total household income.
- Paying down the principal on your mortgage is a risk-free investment.

BUILDING YOUR RETIREMENT PLAN

Simply dreaming of that idyllic retirement and hoping it will work out won't get it done. Hope is not a strategy; a lot of planning, a disciplined approach and sometimes sacrifice are involved. Many people spend more time planning a vacation than they do thinking about their finances. It's not that spending time on planning their vacation is a bad thing; it is the lack of planning for their financial future that is disturbing.

The good news is that once your plan is in place, spending one hour, three or four times a year, should be enough to keep your plans up-to-date. You can tackle this project on your own but in many cases the novelty wears off, the tasks become drudgery and important matters get set aside.

If the task seems overwhelming, a financial advisor can walk you through the whole process and help you lay out a workable strategy. By doing some groundwork ahead of time, a discussion with an advisor should run smoothly and quickly.

Begin with a Vision

The expectations of a retirement lifestyle can be as ambitious as a second home in Palm Springs or as modest as an apartment close to the grandchildren.

When developing a retirement plan, **begin with a vision** of what you would like retirement to be. The vision will probably change over time and the plan could also exceed or fall short of expectations, but there are four simple questions that can be used as a starting point.

- **Who will you spend retirement with?** – While you may envision spending your retirement with your spouse, you might also be single and plan to retire on your own. Some retirees may still have dependents for whom they are responsible. The question of who you will spend your retirement with will affect what you do and what expenses you will face.

- **What will you do in retirement?** – While you might envision a simple retirement close to family and friends, you may also want to travel or continue your education. You need to think of your daily routine, regardless of whether it is simple or full of activity. It should be a rewarding lifestyle that brings you a sense of satisfaction. Too many people think only of what they won't be doing (going to work) rather than what they will be doing with their time.

- **Where will you live?** - Will you be staying in your current home; will you be downsizing or renting; will you want a vacation property? These are all questions you need to ask yourself. You need to estimate the costs, the access to healthcare, any tax implications of a move and a variety of other factors.

- **What is your state of health?** – The cost of health care for retirees can be higher than for the younger generations. The current condition of your health and the future prospects of your health are important considerations. Does your family medical history raise any warning signs? There are no guarantees when it comes to the state of our health so plans should keep our health in mind.

'When Can I Retire?' by Andrew Allentuck provides some great insight into lifestyle choices in retirement. Take the time to read it, if you can. Your chances of making good decisions improve with the amount of knowledge you gather.

How much do you need to retire?

Once you have decided on your vision for retirement, the next step is to calculate how to fulfil this vision. While the first question is often "How much do I need to retire?", it is a question that can't be answered without having more information.

There are five major variables to consider and each has a significant impact on what the final number will be. You have some control over these first two factors:

- Knowing the level of income you want in retirement – your retirement budget.
- The age at which you hope to retire.

Three factors are out of your control and reasonable assumptions must be used:

- The estimated rate of return you expect to achieve on your investments.
- The rate of inflation (annual increase in the cost of living) during your lifetime.
- Your life expectancy.

The following guidelines can help you determine an appropriate number for each of these variables. While some of them are out of your control, you still need to make reasonable estimates or assumptions.

Your retirement budget

While many financial plans provide detailed analyses of pension benefits, accumulation of capital and rates of return, it is all for naught if the basic assumption of income requirements is inaccurate.

Some investors calculate their retirement income needs as a percentage of current income, while others have the goal of maintaining a level of income in retirement that is 'about average' or maybe a little better. Both of these approaches are unfocused and lack specifics. There is a better way.

Take the time to prepare a retirement budget; you only have to do it once. After that it becomes a matter of adjustments as your vision for retirement changes. It is definitely worth the extra effort and you will then have meaningful data on which to base your decisions.

We can look at the three approaches in more detail.

First approach – Percentage of Income

One rule of thumb that is commonly mentioned in financial publications for estimating your retirement income requirements is **the 70% factor**. In other words, 70% of the income you earn in your final year of employment is appropriate for your first year of retirement.

The logic behind using some kind of a discount over earned income is that the retiree likely no longer has a mortgage payment; there are no contributions to RRSP accounts, no Canada Pension Plan contributions and no EI contributions. Other expenses, such as children's education, may also disappear.

While the percentage of income approach is better than not making an estimate, it has its shortcomings.

The problem lies in the fact that few of us know what we will be making in our final year of employment. If you wait long enough until you do know, it will be too late to make any changes to your retirement plans.

This approach also fails to take into account the kind of lifestyle someone may expect to have in retirement. Low wage earners may have grandiose dreams, while a highly-paid professional may seek a more simple life.

A study by Statcan found that people who earned over $70,000 tended to retire on about 45% of their pre-retirement income, while those who earned between $40,000 and $50,000 per year retired on about 59% of their retirement income. Some financial advisors recommend a number as high as 80% of pre-retirement income as an appropriate guideline for retirement income. That number may serve the advisor's goals of managing a large amount of assets better than it serves the client's goal of having adequate savings for retirement.

Money and income is only part of retirement. The broad brush of a 70% factor does not encourage someone to visualize their lifestyle in retirement. Thinking about how each day will unfold and what the routine will be for the next 20 or 30 years can make a prospective retiree pause. If you use a percentage of pre-retirement income, you gloss over this important aspect.

Second approach – Average retirement incomes

With the lack of a better guideline, the question is often asked, "What does everyone else live on in retirement?" It's a question that is worth looking at.

The chart below provides a general historical picture of the *average after-tax income* from 1991 to 2010 for elderly families, elderly males and elderly females. For the purposes of comparison, the incomes have been adjusted to 2010 dollars to account for inflation.

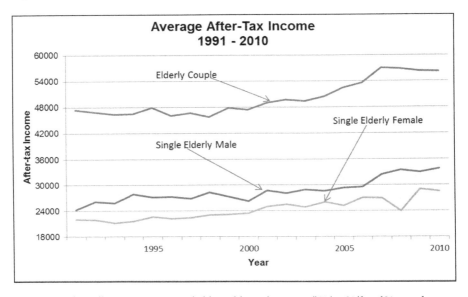

Source: http://www.statcan.gc.ca/tables-tableaux/sum-som/l01/cst01/famil21a-eng.htm

As with using percentage of income, using these averages also has its shortcomings.

A retiree who has to pay rent may have higher expenses for shelter than someone who has a home that is mortgage-free. And a retiree in Toronto or Vancouver may have much higher expenses than someone who lives in small town Canada.

You may also want to ask yourself, 'What will the average income be for retirees when I am ready to retire?' It could be far different from what it is today.

When comparing the historical income of retired Canadians, it is important to note that each year inflation results in a cost of living that is higher than the year before. At an average inflation rate of 2.25% per year, the annual cost of living would increase by 25% in just 10 years.

The couple who project income needs of $45,000 in 2010 would need over $56,000 in 2020 to achieve the same standard of living. Inflation is a factor that is often given minimal attention and which can be a dangerous oversight. Where does the extra $11,000 per year come from if you haven't planned for it? Always apply an inflation factor when estimating retirement income needs.

Using a percentage of pre-retirement income or the average income of retired Canadians are vague approaches. It is obvious that finding a method to more accurately estimate your income needs in retirement would be valuable in the retirement planning process.

Third approach – A personalized retirement budget

The first two approaches do provide some broad guidelines but the estimates can vary so much that they are barely useful in calculating an appropriate retirement income. They fall far short in recognizing the **varying needs and expectations** of each individual and the only person who can measure those factors is you.

The process of developing a retirement budget requires some time and thought; however, once it is complete you will have a solid foundation on which to begin. It must correspond to your vision of retirement. For each budget item, an annual expenditure must be estimated. The good news is there are guidelines available for most budget items. Sample budgets can also help to raise awareness of items that have been overlooked.

The following example provides more detailed retirement budgets that illustrate the wide range of incomes of various individuals.

- The ***first budget*** is the hypothetical budget of a retired couple who have **minimal income requirements** and who live in a house that is mortgage-free.
- The ***second budget*** illustrates a couple who desire an ***above average lifestyle*** and who expect to be renting their accommodation in retirement.

Their income needs will be very different from one another.

There are an infinite number of variations that can be used as examples. The point is that there is no one number that applies to everyone and that is why it is important to define your own vision and develop your own budget.

Item	Minimal Income Budget for a Couple	Above Average Income Budget for a Couple
Mortgage or rent	$0.00	$18,000.00
Property taxes	$3,000.00	$0.00
Maintenance, utilities and insurance	$3,600.00	$900.00
Cable, Internet, Telephone, Mobile phone	$1,500.00	$2,000.00
Groceries	$7,200.00	$9,000.00
Vehicle payments and/or public transportation expense	$3,000.00	$6,000.00
Car license & insurance	$1,200.00	$1,500.00
Car fuel, oil & maintenance	$1,500.00	$3,500.00
Household expenses	$600.00	$900.00
Dry cleaning, laundry, etc.	$600.00	$900.00
Personal care – salon expenses	$900.00	$1500.00
Clothing	$1,500.00	$2,500.00
Pharmacy, medical, dental and medical insurance	$2,000.00	$3000.00
Entertainment – movies, restaurant dining, etc.	$900.00	$1,800.00
Alcohol & tobacco	$300.00	$1,000.00
Recreation – golf, tennis, gym	$1,000.00	$3,000.00
Travel	$3,000.00	$9,000.00
Miscellaneous, gifts, etc.	$1,500.00	$3,000.00
Total for two people	$33,300.00	$67,000.00
Taxes	$2,700.00	$11,000.00
Total gross income required	$36,000.00	$78,000.00

With the completion of a budget, a more specific goal has been established and the first step in developing a retirement investment plan has been taken. The plan might have to be revised several times before it becomes feasible but it does provide you with a solid starting point. The compromises might include changing your expectations for the future or making sacrifices in your current lifestyle.

Your customized retirement budget will be the major factor used in determining how much you will have to accumulate for retirement. It is the foundation of all your retirement planning and it is wise to put a lot of thought into it.

Complex calculations involving RRSP contributions, rates of return and pension benefits are meaningless unless you know what your income requirements will be. Despite this, so many financial planning analyses will oversimplify this part of the process and use a factor like 70% of income, without knowing whether it is even remotely accurate in assessing your needs and objectives.

Choosing a retirement age – a critical decision

Those who choose to retire early not only have to make their savings last for a longer period of time, but they also have fewer years in which to accumulate those increased savings. Working even one extra year can allow for one more year of contributions to your savings, one more year of growth for those savings and one year less in which you will be drawing income from those savings.

In addition, many government benefits won't be available until at least age 60, and even then they would be reduced benefits. Recent legislation will change the qualifying age for Old Age Security to 67 years by 2029. The discount on CPP benefits for those who withdraw before age 65 has also increased. In the future, those who choose to begin drawing CPP at age 60 will have their annual benefits reduced by 36%. It is a big price to pay for early retirement.

With the changes to legislation it is clear that we are being encouraged to postpone retirement to age 65 or later. The financial incentives are significant.

Working a year or two longer can make a substantial difference to the level of income you can draw in your retirement years and it may provide you with the freedom to enjoy a far more comfortable lifestyle. It may even allow you to pursue dreams that once seemed out of reach.

Choose your preferred retirement age carefully. You may have to run several projections to find a retirement that suits your financial situation and provides the compromise between earlier retirement and higher income. It is important that you give this decision serious consideration.

Age of Retirement – detailed analysis

The age at which you retire is one of the few variables under your control. Sixty-five was commonly used as the ideal age for retirement, perhaps because it coincided with some of the mandatory retirement ages that were put in place years ago. It also fits in nicely with Canada Pension Plan (CPP) and Old Age Security (OAS) benefits.

"A Portrait of Seniors in Canada" published by Statcan in 2006 http://www.statcan.gc.ca/pub/89-519-x/89-519-x2006001-eng.pdf discovered the following trends:

> *"The median age of retirement has fallen dramatically in the past two decades. From the mid 1970s to the mid 1980s, it hovered around age 65. But in the late 1980s, it started dropping quickly, and continued to do so until hitting a low of 60.6 in 1997, and then fluctuating around that level in subsequent years.*
>
> *"This decline was most likely initiated in 1987 by lowering the minimum age at which one could begin to draw benefits from the Canada Pension Plan – from age 65 to 60, with reduced benefits."*

In addition, vibrant investment markets that existed during the last decade of the twentieth century created the illusion that these markets could easily support a long and pleasant retirement.

An advertising campaign launched by London Life several years also may have helped to change perceptions with the catchy slogan of 'Freedom Fifty-Five'. It was a campaign that caught on quickly and it planted unrealistic expectations in the minds of many. Like the books that promised an easy path to fame and fortune, the advertising campaign told people what they wanted to hear. It could be done and it wasn't that difficult. A long and idyllic retirement was within our grasp.

The following chart taken from that study shows the trend of retirement age among Canadians since 1976. As a society we never got close to Freedom 55 and, in fact, that dream seems to be getting farther away.

Source: Statistics Canada, Cansim Table 282-0051

LIFE EXPECTANCY

Another variable is life expectancy and many people make the mistake of underestimating how long they expect to live.

Despite the cruelty of cancer, the tragedy of Alzheimer's and the sudden grief caused by a fatal heart attack or stroke, Canadians are generally living longer. This admirable trend has had its consequences. It means our retirement money must now last longer.

Those who expected retirement to last only ten or fifteen years may find that they are living longer than expected and their retirement portfolio has been depleted. In that situation there aren't many alternatives other than accepting an austere lifestyle.

When we are young we may attach very little importance to our lifestyle at 80 years old but that will change as we approach that age. More Canadians than ever are active well into their eighties. They golf, dance, travel, go to concerts and want modern, comfortable accommodation. Independent living accommodation can cost $3000 per month per person or more. Life does not necessarily get less expensive later in life and we are living longer.

When creating a retirement plan, choosing an appropriate life expectancy is an important decision. It is one more of those variables over which there is little control. Underestimating your life expectancy can lead to an inadequate commitment to savings, resulting in an impoverished existence and loss of dignity in a person's final years.

The best alternative is to refer to reliable research that has been done on the subject. A website with a lot of valuable information is www.worldlifeexpectancy.com.

Canadian females who were 60 years of age in 2011 had an average life expectancy of 86 years, while for males the corresponding numbers are 79 years and 83 years. In other words, approximately one-half of the females currently aged 60 will live beyond age 86 and one-half of the males currently aged 60 will live beyond age 83.

There are a wide number of variables and consulting the World Life Expectancy website can be helpful. For those who find the website overwhelming, a rule of thumb for both men and women can be applied for retirement planning purposes.

- Women may want to use a minimum life expectancy of about 90 years.
- Men may want to use a minimum a life expectancy of about 87 years.

If those numbers look higher than the average life span it is because they are. Using a higher number than the average life expectancy helps to build in a cushion. Sound planning would be to consult the life expectancy tables and bump that number up by three or four years just to have an insurance policy against good health. That might sound a bit strange but when someone is in their 80s there is very little opportunity to supplement their retirement income from other sources if they live longer than expected.

Rate of Return

One of the misconceptions that plagues many investors is the actual rate of return they will be able to achieve on investments during their retirement. For years, 10% seemed to be the standard. It is easy to calculate and seemed well within reach given the performance of the stock market and equity mutual funds during the 1980s and 1990s.

This is the one assumption that often draws the most attention and is likely to be the one that is the most inaccurate. Investors can become fixated on rate of return when it is the one over which they have the least influence. It is counter-productive and can lead to poor investment choices.

Over-estimating your future rate of return and then hoping your investments will achieve those lofty expectations is a recipe for disaster. It leads to underfunded portfolios as you rely more on the returns your investments achieve and less on the contributions you make.

Everyone is susceptible to this trap. Numerous pension plans at both the government and corporate level are underfunded because their expectations for growth were too optimistic. In many cases, corporations don't have the money to top up the plans and some governments may not be able to honour their pension commitments. There is no magic pool of capital to fund some of these payments as they now stand.

The dilemma of an underfunded retirement plan can lead to poor decisions. You may be tempted to abandon your strategy and become far more aggressive than your situation dictates. In an effort to make up for less than expected returns, some investors take on more risk in their portfolios than they should, often unknowingly. Do not fall into that trap.

The projected rate of return for a portfolio will depend on its asset mix which is something that needs to be discussed in more detail. For the purposes of estimating rates of return it is sufficient at this point to assume that more conservative portfolios should have lower rates of return over long periods of time and more aggressive portfolios should have higher rates of return.

An example of unrealistic returns can be found in 'The Wealthy Barber'. Author David Chilton is careful not to predict rates of return for a portfolio, but returns like 15%, 12% and 10% are alluded to in the whimsical conversations.

These conversations imply that rates of return at these levels were possible. In the days when the book was written, it didn't seem so far-fetched. North American and European stock markets were in the middle of the greatest bull market (period of high growth) that anyone had ever seen. Double digit returns were being achieved year after year.

Since the beginning of the new millennium, the story has been far different and stock markets in 2012 were barely any higher than they were twelve years ago. Investors who had expected the double digit returns may have been more than sorely disappointed; they may have faced financial hardship. Unrealistic expectations can lead to unintended consequences.

So which numbers more accurately reflect what the future might hold? Is it the double digit returns of the 80s and 90s or is it the disappointment of the first twelve years of the new millennium? The truth is that both situations must be considered.

Pension plans use consulting firms and actuaries to estimate future returns on their plans. These estimates use discount rates which in turn are used to determine whether a pension plan has adequate funds to meet future needs. Individual investors don't have the same kind of information at their fingertips but a little bit of basic research can be revealing.

Setting Expectations

One of the biggest challenges facing investors and advisors is setting the level of expectations for portfolio performance. It is not only the expectations regarding the rate of return that need to be established, it is also necessary to establish the expectations of the consistency of the returns. This consistency (or inconsistency) in the returns from one year to the next represents the volatility of your portfolio.

If there was a golden age for the individual investor, it was probably in the twenty-year period from 1980 to 2000. Without going into all of the reasons behind why it happened, stock markets experienced unprecedented growth and the average investor jumped on board. The popularity of mutual funds exploded as they offered investors an easy way to access the market.

That period shaped the expectations for many and some still cling to the belief that those were normal years. They believe what we have experienced since then is an aberration. History tells us otherwise. In the long term, markets have experienced long periods of above average growth followed by long periods of below average growth.

Both periods have to be accounted for when trying to estimate what long term returns might be. Only taking the optimistic side or the pessimistic side leads to disappointment or missed opportunities. Using a twenty-year time frame on which to base estimates misses a good part of the last bull market which began in the mid 1980s. Using a ten-year time frame misses all of it.

A longer term is required to measure the full historical impact of long bull markets and long bear markets. A fifty-year time frame is sure to include all kinds of market conditions and allow us to draw conclusions using a vast amount of data.

An excellent source for all kinds of financial and tax information is www.taxtips.ca. It can take some time to find what you are looking for but the information is exceptional. Coincidentally, they provide information on market returns and inflation.

Historical Long Term Trends

When considering what long term returns might be, it is important to factor in the good times as well as the bad times over a complete cycle, which is often about 30 years in length. Using a shorter time period on which to base your estimates can skew your perception to being overly optimistic or overly pessimistic.

The following chart illustrates long term periods of growth followed by long term periods of stagnant returns. Focusing only on the growth or only on the stagnation would give you a false impression of how the markets deliver returns to investors. Those contrasting periods of time result in emotional highs and lows that need to be moderated in order for you to make rational investment decisions.

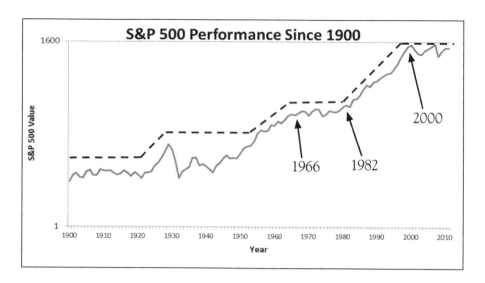

Those who based their rate of return expectations on the average annual stock market returns from 1982 to 2000 would have been severely disappointed on the returns since that time. A better choice would have been to use the average annual rate of return from 1966 to 2000 which would take into account both a long bull market and a long bear market that lasted 35 years in total. By doing this you are factoring in both the good times and the bad into your calculations.

Real rates of return

The real rate of return you achieve on an investment is the amount by which your actual (nominal) rate of return exceeds inflation. We have already seen the danger of using short term returns as a guide for estimating long term returns. It is important to consider the returns achieved over a long market cycle to ensure that you are including periods of average growth, above average growth and below average growth in determining a reasonable estimate.

There is no fifty-year information on Canadian stock market returns but the US market, as measured by the S&P 500 index, achieved average annual returns of 9.6% in Canadian dollars for the period ending December 31, 2012. Over that same period of time, the long term Canadian bond market achieved annual returns of 7.6%.

In that same 50 year time period, inflation averaged 4.1% per year. That means the US equity market provided returns that were 5.5% over and above inflation, while the long term Canadian bond market provided returns that were 3.5% over and above inflation.

Rates of Return to December 31, 2012					
	1 year	5 years	10 years	20 years	50 years
Type of Investment	Avg. Annual Return	Avg. Annual Return	Avg. Annual Return	Avg. Annual Return	Avg. Annual Return
Cdn 3 month T-bills	1.0%	1.0%	2.1%	3.3%	6.2%
Cdn Govt Bonds 1 to 3 year	1.1%	1.6%	2.58%	4.0%	6.6%
Cdn Govt Bonds over 10 years	2.3%	3.4%	4.0%	5.4%	7.6%
S&P/TSX (Cdn) Index (formerly TSE300)	4.0%	-1.1%	6.6%	6.8%	n/a
Nikkei 225 Index in Cdn$	9.1%	-1.0%	2.4%	-0.3%	n/a
S&P 500 (US) Index in Cdn$	13.5%	1.8%	2.3%	7.2%	9.6%
European stocks in Cdn$	17.3%	-3.6%	4.1%	7.6%	n/a
Emerging markets stocks in Cdn$	16.0%	-0.5%	11.7%	7.8%	n/a
Canadian Consumer Price Index All Items (inflation)	0.8%	1.6%	1.9%	1.8%	4.1%

Source: www.taxtips.ca

For the purposes of estimating long returns in their retirement plans, investors are well advised to use a rate on equities that is 5% over inflation and a rate on bonds that is 3% over inflation. These two numbers are far more relevant than an arbitrary number that has no relationship to the cost of living. Returns of 10% may be great but if inflation is 12% the investor is still going backwards.

Sideways markets

There are always temptations in the investment world and those temptations may lead investors to the asset class with the highest returns over the long term. In this case, equities far surpassed bonds in terms of performance over the past fifty years but in the past ten years the roles have been reversed.

Using the same source of data, www.taxtips.ca, the ten-year returns for the period ending December 31, 2012 on the S&P 500 were 2.3% per year. When inflation is factored into the equation, 1.9% per year in purchasing power was lost. The inflation adjusted return was only 0.4% *per year!*

Yes, the stock market has provided superior long term returns, but it is not always the best place to invest and no one has yet discovered a way to determine if stocks or bonds will be the best performer in any given year. The best that can be done is to allocate investments prudently among different types of investments or asset classes.

Those who advocate sticking to a pure equity portfolio because 'the stock market always bounces back in the long run' may have failed to explain what the long run really means. For many, ten years is the long run. What would the reaction be if investors were told it would take 15 or 20 years for their portfolios to bounce back?

Inconsistent returns

While these long term returns are useful for making projections, they create an illusion that the returns will consistently fall somewhere close to these numbers. Nothing could be further from the truth. Returns will swing wildly from one year to the next and investors must prepare themselves for this psychological roller coaster.

Single asset portfolios that include only equities will experience more wild swings than portfolios with multiple complementary assets. The psychological roller coaster will be much less exciting.

Summary

If equities are expected to earn 5.0% per year over inflation and it is assumed that inflation will average about 2.5% per year, the expected gross return on equities over the long term would be 7.5%. Similarly, if bonds are expected to earn 3% over inflation, the expected gross return over the long term would be 5.5%.

These numbers may be far below what some investors hope to achieve but they are based on long term historical data. Even using this data, the return expectations may be optimistic. The danger for investors is that they base their savings on the expectation of higher returns only to fall short. It is far better to be conservative with estimated returns, and if they are exceeded it makes for a more comfortable or earlier retirement.

Long term historical rates of return will change over time as economies move through cycles of expansion and recession, so the basis for making rate of return assumptions also changes. It is good practice to review rate of return assumptions once a year to determine if they are still reasonable. A change in assumptions might require a change in strategy but making small, timely changes is far better than a nasty surprise when retirement is just around the corner.

The Effect of Investor Behaviour on Portfolio Returns

Although it is worthwhile discussing the returns provided by the various markets, as well as the returns achieved by the various mutual fund managers, even those numbers may be overly optimistic. One reason for that is investor psychology. As a group, we tend to invest more readily only after the markets have gone up and shown a semblance of stability for a period of time. On the other hand, we tend to sell when we are disappointed because the markets have corrected.

Dalbar Inc. is an organization that develops standards and measurement systems designed to improve the quality of communications and service in the healthcare and financial services industries. You can learn more about Dalbar at www.dalbar.com.

They quantified the effect of irrational investor behaviour in a study published in April 2012. In that study Dalbar found that over the twenty-year period ending in December 2011 the ***average investor underperformed*** the equity index (S&P 500) by 4.32% per year and underperformed the bond index (Barclay's Aggregate Bond Index) by 5.56% per year.

You can access Dalbar's reports from their website at http://www.qaib.com/public/default.aspx

The biggest challenge facing investors in their attempts to achieve reasonable returns on their investment portfolios is not minimizing fees and it is not trying to pick the next best stock or mutual fund; it is overcoming our emotions that tell us to buy only when we are comfortable and sell when we are uncomfortable.

The danger in averages

Using average returns may be a suitable way to define long term targets but returns are inconsistent from one year to the next. Those seeking a 5% annual return may see a gain of 15% one year, a loss of 10% the next and a gain of 12% in the third year. While the average return will be somewhere close to 5%, it won't feel like that to the investor. It will feel like a roller coaster and it will be difficult to make objective investment decisions.

Emotion is something that is often forgotten in the mathematical world of financial planning and is almost impossible to quantify.

Where do you fit?

The next challenge facing the investor lies in determining what category they fall into. In many cases investors have an idea of which category reflects their personal situation. If it is chosen honestly, then the projected rate of return associated with that category provides a reasonable starting point.

This process in itself faces problems. First, some investors have no idea whether they should be conservative, growth oriented or somewhere in between. Second, even when some feel comfortable in classifying their tolerance to risk, they don't know how to equate that profile to a long term rate of return. The result can be the expectation of a rate of return that has no basis in fact.

As a guideline, investors might want to consider the following long term returns based on the asset mix that is appropriate for them. That asset mix (which will be discussed in more detail later) may be labelled and loosely estimated as follows:

Risk Tolerance Profile	Rate of Return	Predictability Of Returns	Volatility
Risk averse	3.0%	Highest	Lowest
Conservative	4.0%	↕	↕
Income Oriented	5.0%		
Moderate	6.0%		
Growth Oriented	7.0%	Lowest	Highest

While these numbers seem surprisingly low for some, they are based on the long term historical returns of various asset classes. Combining the various investments available to the average investor into a mix that suits their tolerance to risk provides guidelines as to what they should expect over the long term, irrational behaviour aside.

Of course, the tables are backwards looking. In other words, they reflect what has already happened and there can be no assurances that history will repeat itself. Still, using some kind of guideline is better than using none at all.

The whole process of choosing an appropriate rate of return to use in retirement projections may seem like overkill but it isn't. It may be the one variable that investors over-estimate more than any other and it can lead to a serious shortfall in the quest to accumulate investment assets for retirement.

The actual rate of return you will achieve will depend on the investment choices you make and those choices should fit with your investment profile.

Equally important to the rate of return you are earning is the amount of capital you are able to accumulate. That accumulation comes from a combination of **deposits and growth**. Sometimes one has to compensate for the other.

It would be hard to find many people who want to save everything for retirement and not enjoy life now. The question is how to approach the problem. A balance has to be struck and compromises made.

The Effects of Inflation

The challenge that arises with a retirement budget is that it usually approximates expenses in today's dollars because no one knows for certain what costs will be in the future. It is clear that someone who wants to retire with an income equivalent of $30,000 in today's dollars will need much more than that in the future. Keep in mind that inflation doesn't end on the day we retire. It continues to affect our purchasing power throughout life.

The compromise is estimating how much more everything will cost in the future. In other words, it is estimating inflation. That is one of many reasons why **all financial plans are an inexact science**. We can look at history and try to draw some conclusions but it is impossible to say how accurate they will be.

Using historical data is one tool you can use when choosing an inflation rate for your financial plan. It's not perfect but it is far better than ignoring the effects of inflation.

The consumer price index (CPI) measures the cost of a hypothetical basket of goods and services used by the average Canadian. It includes such items as the cost of accommodation, food, clothing, transportation, health care, consumer items and so on.

The year to year change in CPI is how we measure the overall cost of living increase or inflation.

Everyone will have their own unique basket of goods and services so it becomes impossible to measure each unique basket and the price changes within that basket. The compromise is to measure the change in the average basket and allow each individual to estimate whether the change in their basket will differ from the average.

The changes in CPI, therefore, are meant to be used as a guideline on which to base your own personal assumptions.

The Statcan website provides a wealth of information on this topic. The average annual rate of inflation over a 20 year time period in Canada is illustrated in the table below.

Consumer Price Index in Canada – 1993 to 2012					
Year	Index Value	Percent Increase	Year	Index Value	Percent Increase
1993	85.6	1.9	2003	102.8	2.8
1994	85.7	0.1	2004	104.7	1.8
1995	87.6	2.2	2005	107.0	2.2
1996	88.9	1.5	2006	109.1	2.0
1997	90.4	1.7	2007	111.5	2.2
1998	91.3	1.0	2008	114.1	2.3
1999	92.9	1.8	2009	114.4	0.3
2000	95.4	2.7	2010	116.5	1.8
2001	97.8	2.5	2011	119.9	2.9
2002	100	2.2	2012	121.7	1.5

Source: Statistics Canada

Over the most recent 20-year time period which ended on December 31, 2012, inflation, as measured by the increase in CPI (consumer price index), increased by approximately 2.00% per year. A look at the table will quickly tell you that a basket of goods that cost $86 in 1993 would cost almost $122 in 2012.

Even with the modest inflation that we have experienced in Canada, our cost of living has increased by over 42% in the past 20 years.

A more complete history of inflation can be seen on the Statcan website at http://www.statcan.gc.ca/tables-tableaux/sum-som/l01/cst01/econ46a-eng.htm and it is worth examining closely. There have been 10-year periods where inflation has averaged over 6% per year. At those rates the cost of living would have risen about 70% in that time period!

Under-estimating inflation can be as critical as over-estimating returns when putting together a retirement plan. The two actually go hand in hand. Using a rate of 2.25% per year is slightly higher than recent history but lower than the average rate over the past 50 years.

A word of caution is advised. Poor policy decisions by governments and central banks, combined with unfavourable economic circumstances, can result in much higher inflation than we have recently experienced.

The table below illustrates how an inflation rate of 2.25% would affect a retirement budget. A typical retirement lasts more than 20 years so I have included the budget in today's dollars, what it would be in the first year of retirement, and what it would be in the twentieth year of retirement. The numbers get very big, very quickly.

Years to Retirement	Inflation Factor at 2.25%	Retirement Budget Today's Dollars	Retirement Budget 1st year of Retirement	Retirement Budget 20th year of Retirement
5	1.12	$50,000	$56,000	$85,500
10	1.25	$35,000	$62,500	$95,500
15	1.40	$50,000	$70,000	$106,500
20	1.56	$50,000	$78,000	$119,000
25	1.74	$50,000	$87,000	$132,500
30	1.94	$50,000	$95,500	$145,500
35	2.17	$50,000	$108,500	$165,500

Those **most susceptible to high inflation** are the risk-averse and conservative investors. In an effort to protect their capital or principal, they put their purchasing power at risk. It is important to remember that if rates of return are lower than inflation, the purchasing power of a portfolio declines.

In 2011 the rate of inflation was measured at 2.9% while a one-year GIC purchased at the beginning of the year may have carried a yield of 1.5%. While the investor would have had more money at the end of the year, it would have purchased less. Prices had gone up faster than the value of the investment and purchasing power would have been lost.

Inflation is the silent killer of retirement plans. Every year it eats away at purchasing power and the effects cannot be overstated.

Sources of Income

For almost every Canadian, retirement income will come from more than one source. There are government benefits, such as CPP and OAS, there are employer sponsored pension plans and there are personal savings in the form of RRSPs, TFSAs and investment accounts. For others there may be business income, rental income or part time employment.

Statcan data illustrates the various sources of income relied upon by seniors in the past.

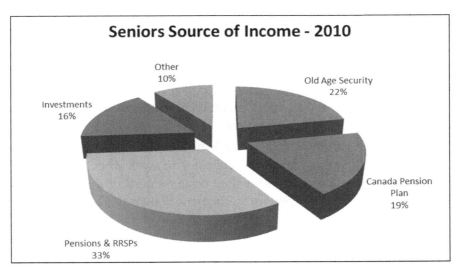

Source: (CANSIM Table 202-0407). Ottawa: Statistics Canada, 2012
http://www4.hrsdc.gc.ca/.3ndic.1t.4r@-eng.jsp?iid=27

All of these possible sources of income must be taken into account when trying to determine how much of that retirement income will come from personal savings. At the same time, each of these sources of income will be influenced by a variety of factors.

Canada Pension Plan (CPP)

As of January 2, 2013, the maximum monthly benefit available at 65 years of age was $1012, while the average benefit paid was about $530 per month.

The general theory behind CPP is that those who worked continuously to age 65 during their adult years will collect up to 25% of their annual employment income each year. You can begin to draw reduced benefits as early as age 60 or defer drawing benefits until as late as age 70. Of course, there are a number of restrictions, exceptions and limitations, but the Service Canada website (http://www.servicecanada.gc.ca/eng/isp/cpp/cpptoc.shtml) provides you with the tools to calculate what your CPP benefits might be upon retirement.

Regardless of when you begin to draw your CPP benefits, the amount is adjusted for inflation each year.

Benefits are based on the amount of contribution made and those contributions are based on your pensionable earnings up to a yearly maximum (YPME). A person's CPP retirement pension is calculated as 25% of his average pensionable earnings during his contributory period. The contributory period starts when he turns 18, or 1966, whichever is later. The contributory period ends upon retirement.

You can begin to draw CPP as early as age 60 but recent changes to CPP legislation requires those who continue to work while drawing CPP must still contribute to CPP until they cease to work or until they reach age 70. This is known as the Post Retirement Benefit or PRB.

> *Canadians working outside of Quebec who receive a CPP or QPP retirement pension will begin making CPP contributions toward the PRB on* **January 1, 2012**. *The benefit will be paid to you the following year, starting in 2013.*
>
> *These contributions are mandatory for CPP and QPP retirement pension recipients aged 60 to 65. If you are at least 65 but under 70 years of age, you can choose not to contribute.*

You can learn more about CPP benefits at: http://www.servicecanada.gc.ca/eng/isp/cpp/prb/index.shtml.

Yearly Maximum Pensionable Earnings Basis for CPP Calculation

Year	Earnings	Year	Earnings	Year	Earnings
2013	$51,100	1997	$35,800	1981	$14,700
2012	$50,100	1996	$35,400	1980	$13,100
2011	$48,300	1995	$34,900	1979	$11,700
2010	$47,200	1994	$34,400	1978	$10,400
2009	$46,300	1993	$33,400	1977	$9,300
2008	$44,900	1992	$32,200	1976	$8,300
2007	$43,700	1991	$30,500	1975	$7,400
2006	$42,100	1990	$28,900	1974	$6,600
2005	$41,100	1989	$27,700	1973	$5,600
2004	$40,500	1988	$26,500	1971	$5,500
2003	$39,900	1987	$25,900	1970	$5,400
2002	$39,100	1986	$25,800	1969	$5,300
2001	$38,300	1985	$23,400	1968	$5,200
2000	$37,600	1984	$20,800	1967	$5,100
1999	$37,400	1983	$18,500	1966	$5,000
1998	$36,900	1982	$16,500	1965	n/a

Source: www.servicecanada.gc.ca

The calculation required to determine your benefits is not straightforward.

In order to qualify for maximum benefits, your maximum pensionable earnings would have to be greater than, or equal to, the amount listed in the table in each of the years you were eligible for employment since age 18. For example, an individual born in 1952 would be eligible to make contributions beginning in 1970. But some low earning years can be disregarded.

Starting in 2012, you can drop up to 7.5 years of your lowest earnings from your calculations. This may result in an increase to your benefit amount. In 2014, this will increase again to up to 8 years of your lowest earnings from the calculation. The actual number of years that you can drop is based on the number of years in which you made contributions.

You can set up an account with Service Canada to view and print a history of your earnings and contributions to the Canada Pension Plan. You can also review estimates of benefits you may be eligible to receive.

Early withdrawal

If you choose to retire before age 65 and begin to draw your CPP benefits immediately upon retirement, the CPP payments are reduced. The earliest age at which you can begin to draw CPP is 60.

The following table illustrates the impact of drawing your benefits early.

Approximate Discounts for Early Withdrawal								
Withdrawal Age	Year of Birth							
	1949	1950	1951	1952	1953	1954	1955	1956 & later
60					32.4%	33.6%	34.8%	36.0%
61				25.9%	26.9%	27.9%	28.8%	28.8%
62			19.5%	20.2%	20.9%	21.6%	21.6%	21.6%
63		13.0%	13.5%	14.0%	14.4%	14.4%	14.4%	21.6%
64	6.5%	6.7%	6.9%	7.2%	7.2%	7.2%	7.2%	7.2%

For example, an individual who was born in 1954 and chooses to begin drawing their benefits at age 60 will receive 33.6% per year less than if they had waited until age 65. If their full benefits at age 65 were expected to be $1000 per month, their actual benefits would be $664 per month.

It is one of the prices you pay for early retirement.

General estimate

If you want a very general estimate before receiving your information from Service Canada, you can try the following calculation.

Your average income (in today's dollars) multiplied by 25% will give you an estimate of benefits you may be eligible to receive at age 65. If you worked for fewer than 40 years during that time and/or you begin to draw benefits before age 65, the benefit amounts will be reduced.

Even using this approach, estimating your income from CPP is not a simple task and should be used for only very rough estimates. Your best bet is to establish an account at Service Canada and obtain your historical data. The information you need is available through Service Canada at http://www.servicecanada.gc.ca/eng/isp/common/cricinfo.shtml or you can contact them by phone at 1-800-622-6232 (1–800–O-Canada).

Deferring benefits

Those who choose to defer their first withdrawal until after age 65 will receive increased benefits. The following is a summary of the comments from the Service Canada factsheet at www.servicecanada.gc.ca/eng/isp/pub/factsheets/ISPB-348-11-10_E.pdf:

> ... your monthly CPP retirement pension amount will **increase by a larger percentage** if you take it after age 65. From 2011 to 2013, the Government of Canada will gradually increase this percentage from 0.5% per month (6% per year) to 0.7% per month (8.4% per year). This means that, by 2013, if you start receiving your CPP pension at the age of 70, your pension amount will be 42% more than it would have been if you had taken it at 65.

OLD AGE SECURITY (OAS)

As of January 1, 2012, the maximum OAS benefit available in Canada was $545 per month, with the average benefit paid at approximately $515 per month.

Unlike the Canada Pension Plan, Old Age Security benefits are not reliant on the level of income you earned while you were employed. Most Canadians will qualify for maximum benefits. The exception occurs if you were not a Canadian citizen for your entire adult life.

Pensioners with a net income in excess of approximately $70,000 in 2012 are subject to having some of their OAS benefits clawed back by the government. Those who had a net income in excess of $113,000 in 2012 would have had all of their OAS benefits clawed back.

Changes in OAS Benefits

Recent changes to legislation in Canada will raise the qualification age for OAS benefits to sixty-seven from the current level of age sixty-five.

Canadians born in 1957 or earlier will be able to receive their eligible OAS benefits beginning in the month after they reach age 65. Canadians born in 1963 or later will be able to receive their eligible OAS benefits beginning in the month after they reach age 67. If you were born between 1957 and 1963 you can refer to the following table to determine the age at which you are eligible to begin receiving OAS benefits as the transition is implemented.

Birth Year	1958	1959	1960	1961	1962
Birth Month	Month of First OAS Payment				
January	Feb 2023	Jul 2024	Jan 2026	July 2027	Jan 2029
February	Mar 2023	Sep 2024	Mar 2026	Sep 2027	Mar 2029
March	Apr 2023	Oct 2024	Apr 2026	Oct 2027	Apr 2029
April	Jun 2023	Dec 2024	Jun 2026	Dec 2027	May 2029
May	Jul 2023	Jan 2025	July 2026	Jan 2028	Jun 2029
June	Sep 2023	Mar 2025	Sep 2026	Mar 2028	Jul 2029
July	Oct 2023	Apr 2025	Oct 2026	Apr 2028	Aug 2029
August	Dec 2023	Jun 2025	Dec 2026	Jun 2028	Sep 2029
September	Jan 2024	July 2025	Jan 2027	Jul 2028	Oct 2029
October	Mar 2024	Sep 2025	Mar 2027	Sep 2028	Nov 2029
November	Apr 2024	Oct 2025	Apr 2027	Oct 2028	Dec 2029
December	Jun 2024	Dec 2025	June 2027	Dec 2028	Jan 2030

Source: http://www.servicecanada.gc.ca/eng/isp/oas/changes/index.shtml

The message is clear; you can retire whenever you want but government benefits will be reduced if you retire early.

Additional Issues

The age of retirement must be chosen carefully. The financial benefits of waiting an extra year or two can be surprising. This has to be balanced off with lifestyle decisions or compromises. Rather than going from full employment one day to full retirement the next, one option is a transition into retirement. In the semi-retired phase of this transition, part-time work can supplement income and reduce the erosion of one's life savings.

Delaying retirement for one year allows investments to grow for one additional year and it allows for one additional year of contributions to a savings plan. It also reduces the need for income from investments by one year. Those two factors alone make a big difference, even if it is only a one-year delay.

The challenge is finding a way to compare the various options because of all the factors that come into play. It can be done but it can be a lot of work. A quick way to evaluate your plan and assess the effect of any changes you want to make is to use the retirement planning tools at www.moneypages.com. They can give you a relatively accurate idea of where you stand. From there you may want to pursue a comprehensive financial plan or you may find the Money Pages projections sufficient.

Employer Pension Plans

If you are completing a financial plan using a simple financial planning calculator, you will be asked to provide your pension plan information. For those who are members of an employer-sponsored pension plan, the impact of that plan on the total retirement plan can be significant but pension plans can be very confusing to evaluate.

Part of the problems stems from the fact that there are two completely different types of pension plans. In fact, they are as different as black and white.

The first step is recognizing whether your pension plan is a defined benefit plan or a defined contribution plan. They sound almost the same but they are not. Some corporations may offer defined benefit plans but they are becoming increasingly rare. Or they may offer a defined contribution plan. The same applies to government agencies; the plan offered may be a defined benefit or a defined contribution plan.

Defined Benefit Plans

As the name implies, the benefits received by these pension plan members will be defined or known. The benefits received by the member at retirement are not dependent on how well the investments within the pension plan perform. The benefit is defined and doesn't change whether the pension plan achieves big gains or suffers losses. If the defined benefit is $2500 per month for life, then that is what the pension will pay, regardless of how long the plan member lives or what the rates of return within the plan may be.

For the most part, a defined benefit pension plan provides worry-free income for life; however, there are a couple of caveats. One is the potential bankruptcy of the pension plan's sponsor and the other is inflation.

Potential bankruptcy

If the company sponsoring the pension plan goes into bankruptcy and can no longer make contributions, the viability of the plan could be jeopardized.

It is less likely that governments will default on their pension contributions but even that is not unheard of. Several US municipalities have run into funding problems because of an eroding tax base. Simply raising taxes to maintain funding is not always an option. It can chase taxpayers to more friendly jurisdictions, further eroding the tax base and exacerbating the problem. On the other hand, these municipalities have contractual obligations to their pension plan members.

Disagreements on how to handle these delicate situations can result in long and costly court battles which neither side can win.

Defined benefit plans present a risk for the plan sponsor and are supposedly risk-free for the plan member. The sponsor takes the risk of such things as poor returns and the unexpected longevity of its plan members. No investment decisions are required by the plan members; the outcome is pre-determined.

A pension plan that is not large enough to fund future payment is said to have an unfunded pension liability. The sponsors are responsible for ensuring the pension plan is fully funded and none of this responsibility falls on the plan member. This represents a huge potential cost for the plan sponsor. For this reason, defined benefit plans have become less common as companies and governments seek more cost certainty for their pension liabilities.

In simple terms, a defined benefit plan has a *variable input* or contribution by the plan sponsor and a *pre-determined output* or payment received by the plan member.

Inflation

The second caveat involves inflation. Some defined benefit plans allow for an inflation adjustment factor but many do not. Members of a defined benefit plan that does not include a provision for cost-of-living increases need to be aware that the purchasing power of their pension declines every year. While income remains constant, purchasing power does not.

Defined Contribution Plans

These plans are the mirror image of defined benefit plans. A defined contribution plan has a *pre-determined input* or contribution by the plan sponsor and a *variable output* or payment received by the plan member. In this case, the risk of lower than anticipated returns impacts the plan member rather than the plan sponsor.

Defined contribution plans are gaining favour over defined benefit plans among employers.

In many ways, a defined contribution pension plan is similar to an RRSP. Its characteristics are more comparable to an RRSP than to a defined benefit pension plan. Plan members are given a menu of investments from which to choose in much the same way that an investor chooses investments for their RRSP accounts. The growth of their plan is largely dependent on the performance of the investments they choose. There is no guaranteed income upon retirement.

Because plan members are required to make investment choices, it is important to make the best choices possible. These members face the same challenges as with the RRSP and a similar process for choosing investments should be employed. Using a risk tolerance questionnaire is a good approach.

A defined contribution pension plan also requires a major decision at retirement. Whereas the defined benefit plan simply begins to generate income based on some limited choices, the defined contribution plan ends at retirement. The plan member can have a variety of options from which to choose. These can include purchasing an annuity or selecting a variation of a retirement income fund, such as a:

- Life Income Fund (LIF)
- Prescribed Retirement Income Fund (PRIF)
- Locked-in Retirement Income Fund (LRIF)

The choices available will depend upon the legislation governing the pension.

Even when the choice of investment options is made, there is still another decision. Plan holders may have the option of leaving the investment with the plan administrator or they may be able transfer the management of those assets to their financial advisor.

There are benefits in choosing to transfer your pension assets to your financial advisor upon retirement. It becomes more efficient to monitor all of your holdings and develop an overall investment and withdrawal strategy. It reduces the likelihood of overlap and gaps in your investments which can result in sub-optimal performance and excess volatility. It also ensures that you will receive personalized service from someone who is familiar with your situation.

It is also important to remember that defined contribution plans contain no guarantees with respect to future income. Choosing to remain with the pension plan provider rather than transferring to your financial advisor does not change that.

Sample Financial Plan

At the very least a financial plan should include information about your current situation, the income goals for your retirement, certain financial assumptions, and solutions for any shortfalls. The following example represents what a simple financial plan may look like. It can provide you with a good starting point and if you feel it is necessary, you can have a detailed financial plan prepared.

In a detailed plan additional information would identify yearly income from various sources and take other factors, such as the sale of business, an inheritance, or the downsizing of your home into consideration.

The following table represents a summary of a hypothetical situation where an individual has a slight shortfall in their retirement plan.

Sample Financial Plan – Short Version		
Your information	-	**Self**
Current age		56
Retirement age		63
Current value of all savings		$125,000
Annual contributions to savings		$7,000
Current value of defined contribution pension		$220,000
Annual contributions to defined contribution pension		$8,000
Expected benefits from defined benefit pension		none
Expected monthly CPP benefits at 65		$985
Expected annual living expenses in first year of retirement		$36,000
Assumptions		
Rate of return on investments prior to retirement		5.75%
Rate of return on invests during retirement		4.75%
Annual increase in cost of living		2.25%
Life expectancy		88 years
Calculations		
Estimated value of assets at retirement		$567,500
Estimated gross income required in first year of retirement		$44,800
Estimated CPP in first year of retirement		$11,823
Estimated OAS in first year of retirement		$7,990
Estimated gross income from all sources in retirement		$43,900
Solutions		
Delay your retirement		
OR		
Reduce annual income in retirement by:		$2,900
OR		
Make additional annual contributions prior to retirement of:		$3,880

The following two charts illustrate a hypothetical situation of a couple saving for retirement. They provide a visual representation of how the value of the couple's investments and income change over time. The first chart illustrates how the value of the investments will grow until they reach retirement and how it gradually declines during retirement.

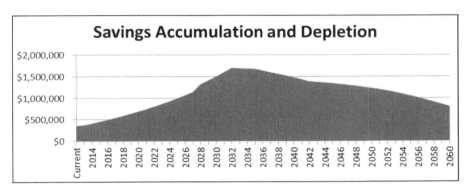

The second chart illustrates the income required in each year of retirement and how that requirement grows with inflation. It also illustrates the sources of income and if there is any shortfall. In this case, there is no shortfall.

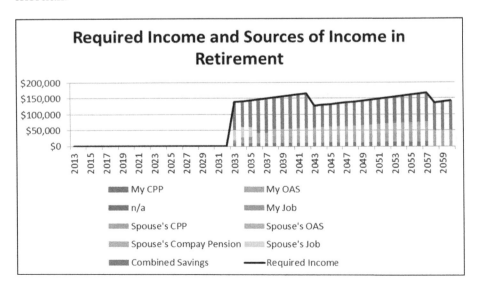

A good financial plan will also allow you to measure your progress and I have included two sample scorecards in the next chapter. They would be a part of your financial plan and allow you to evaluate whether your plan is on track or if adjustments need to be made.

Summary

You should now be aware of many of the variables that can affect your retirement plans but the big question remains. How much capital (money) do you need to accumulate to fund your retirement and avoid the worry of running short of money?

The trick is to find a way to incorporate all of these moving parts into your calculation.

Those who advocate the do-it-yourself approach often overlook the complexities of these various issues that can overwhelm the average investor. Some focus solely on the fees associated with various investment products without considering the many other issues you may face in planning and investing for retirement. Others retreat to low risk, low return investments without considering the long term effects of inflation.

For every story of someone who successfully fired their financial advisor, there will be a story of someone who is thankful they have one.

Assembling all of the required information may seem like a daunting task but reading about it might take longer than doing it. Sitting down with a financial advisor can help. The answers to many of the questions may be right at their fingertips.

Once that information is assembled it must be put to work. Generally speaking, the goal at this stage is to estimate the approximate amount of savings or capital required to fund retirement. Somewhere in all those numbers lies the answer to that question. There are a number of ways to take the next step.

- Attempt to estimate your needs using a calculator, a pencil and a piece of paper.
- Build a spreadsheet using a program like Excel and input your data.

- Use financial planning software or a website that provides financial planning.
- Enlist the services of a fee-based financial planner to develop a comprehensive financial plan.

Some of these approaches will be time consuming and perhaps inaccurate; others may be expensive and provide overwhelming amounts of information. If you have accumulated all the necessary information and want an estimate that provides an uncluttered snapshot of your situation, try the savings requirements estimator at www.moneypages.ca.

It will also provide an estimate of the annual contributions necessary to accumulate the capital required and the results are on one page. Assumptions can be changed easily, making it simple to compare the impact that these changes will have.

None of these estimates, calculations or calculators is meant to replace a comprehensive financial plan. They are merely designed to be tools to help investors get started along the right path by identifying broad targets.

Once realistic targets and solutions are determined, the investor can choose to follow that path or can develop a more detailed financial plan. In either case, you will have developed a standard by which progress can be measured and that measurement will determine a course of action to be followed in the future.

Don't Delay

Many don't start planning the accumulation phase in detail until the distribution phase is almost upon them. When that happens, a sense of urgency can develop. The goal is to start the process early and avoid panic as retirement approaches.

But there are still no guarantees. Factors can conspire to throw the best laid plans offside. Rampant inflation could make the purchasing power of your guaranteed investment certificates almost worthless. Stock market corrections could throw equity portfolios offside. Poor health could see your medical costs soar. No one knows exactly what the future will hold but those reasons should not be an excuse to avoid laying out a blueprint for your retirement.

You can still make reasonable assumptions and provide a margin for error. These assumptions or estimates are the variables used in setting targets for capital accumulation.

If you still want an estimate for the amount of savings you require, here is a very quick rule of thumb if you are retiring at age 65. Estimate the annual income you will need to generate from your investments in retirement. Multiply that number by 20 and the result will be the amount of savings you will need to accumulate. Any income from government benefits, pension plans or other sources will be added to your investment income.

If you retire before age 65, the number will need to be larger.

MONITORING YOUR PROGRESS

PORTFOLIO REVIEWS ARE an important part of any retirement plan but the focus is often placed solely on performance without taking other important factors into consideration.

Part of the problem stems from the fact that many investors don't have a plan in place. In other words, they don't know how much they should have set aside by the time they are thirty-five, forty-five or fifty-five. As a result, they look for other measurements to determine whether or not they are succeeding or falling short.

The easy choice is investment performance. If they are expecting 7% and only achieve 6%, there is disappointment; if they achieve 8%, there is a sense of well-being.

While the rate of return on your investments is the most widely discussed aspect of financial success, it is only half the story; **accumulation of capital** for retirement is the real goal. That accumulation is achieved by a combination of the return you earn on your investments and your personal contributions to your portfolio. The best returns in the world don't do you much good if you have made only token contributions.

A great many Canadians operate without setting that target for the amount of money they need to save. Some avoid the topic altogether and take an ad hoc approach to setting money aside.

Set a target

There are those who advocate that you maximize your RRSP contributions, others suggest you automatically contribute 10% of each paycheque into an investment plan and some say you should do both. Now that TFSAs have been introduced, you now have another account which can be used to save for retirement.

While all of that is fine, it doesn't provide you with any information on whether one or all of these strategies will meet your needs. It is just an open-ended suggestion.

Let's assume that the average income for Canadians in 2008 was about $45,000. The maximum RRSP contribution would be $8100 for someone without a pension plan, a 10% savings plan would be $4500 and the maximum TFSA contribution would be $5000 for a total of $17,600.

On the other hand, according to Statcan, only 50% of Canadians participated in a private retirement savings plan in 2008 and those who did contributed an average of $2700 to their RRSP accounts.

That is a huge discrepancy between what some financial planners suggest for retirement savings and what actually happens in real life. But the real problem is that whether you contribute $15,000 per year or $1,500 per year, you have no idea if you are on target, ahead of target or behind target.

You need to establish some kind of a goal so you can monitor your progress.

In a lot of cases, people may not have been saving enough because they had no idea of what was required. In other cases, some may have been unnecessarily sacrificing their current lifestyle and saving everything for the future. It is important to strike a balance between living well today and saving adequately for the future.

Measure Your Progress

As I mentioned, investors may become fixated on returns rather than the amount of capital they have accumulated. While returns are important, you can agonize over a bad year in the markets when, in reality, your plan might be right on track. Here's an example:

A hypothetical investor has determined he needs to accumulate $500,000 to retire at age 65. He is currently 55 years old, he is contributing $12,000 per year to his portfolio and it is currently worth $200,000. While his rate of return is good in some years and bad in others, he expects to earn 6% per year for the next ten years.

Is he on track to achieve his goal? If he isn't, what does he need to do to get back on track? If he is on track, what should his portfolio be worth when he is 58 or 61 years old? How should he monitor that?

In reality, he only has a vague idea of where he stands.

Keeping a scorecard that compares the actual value of your portfolio with what you need to have is a good way to keep on track. If you are having trouble setting one up or don't know how to get started, your financial advisor can help.

The target year end value and the actual year end value can be easily compared to one another so that discrepancies can be addressed sooner rather than later. The values do not have to match penny for penny. As long as the actual year-end value isn't more than 10% from the target year end value, very little, if anything, needs to be done in the way of adjustments.

Using the example of our 55 year old investor, a scorecard might look something like this:

Sample scorecard for monitoring growth of assets for retirement

Age at Year End	Beginning Value	Growth at 6%	Contributions	Target Year-end Value	Actual Year-end Value
55	$200,000	$12,000	$12,000	$224,000	
56	$224,000	$14,440	$12,000	$249,440	
57	$229,440	$14,966	$12,000	$256,406	
58	$256,406	$15,384	$12,000	$283,790	
59	$283,790	$17,027	$12,000	$312,817	
60	$312,817	$18,769	$12,000	$343,856	
61	$343,856	$20,615	$12,000	$376,471	
62	$376,471	$22,588	$12,000	$411,059	
63	$411,059	$24,663	$12,000	$447,722	
64	$447,722	$26,863	$12,000	$486,585	
65	$486,585	$29,195	$12,000	$527,780	

In this case, the hypothetical investor has realistic expectations. His contributions, along with average annual growth of 6%, should help him achieve his goals. The scorecard helps to monitor whether he is still on track and whether adjustments need to be made to the level of contributions.

There may be instances where the actual year end value is less than the target year end value. The solution is not adopting a more aggressive strategy than what is appropriate; the solution is to contribute more than you had originally planned until you do catch up. It can be a lump sum contribution, or it can simply be an increase in monthly savings, that allows you to catch up over time.

There may also be instances where the actual year end value exceeds the target value. If that is the case, you should resist the temptation to reduce contributions. Murphy's Law could unexpectedly apply and the following year could turn out to be less than expected. A bit of a cushion is never a bad thing.

Once your scorecard is set up, there is very little activity required. Once a year you can sit down and total up the value of your portfolios and input the actual year end value. It might take five minutes per year and is an invaluable tool for helping to keep you on track.

WITHDRAWAL SCORECARD

A *second scorecard* can be set up when you retire. It would be similar to the pre-retirement scorecard but it would monitor the value of your portfolio as you withdraw money for income, rather than when you are adding money for growth. Both help to keep you on track by identifying any adjustments that may be necessary.

In the example below, the investor has chosen to begin withdrawing $30,000 from his portfolio at age 65 and wants to increase that withdrawal each year by 2% to account for inflation. This table does not reflect his total income, only the amount he hopes to withdraw from his portfolio. His other sources of income might be the Canada Pension Plan and Old Age Security.

He has chosen a growth rate of 5% on his portfolio, which is lower than his pre-retirement growth rate because the portfolio will be more conservative and will need to generate income.

Sample scorecard for monitoring assets in retirement

Age at Year End	Beginning Value	Growth At 5%	Withdrawals Adjusted for Inflation	Target Year-end Value	Actual Year-end Value
65	$500,000	$25,000	$30,000	$495,000	
66	$495,000	$24,750	$30,600	$489,150	
67	$489,150	$24,457	$31,212	$482,395	
68	$482,395	$24,120	$31,836	$474,679	
69	$474,679	$23,734	$32,473	$465,940	
60	$465,940	$23,297	$33,122	$456,114	
71	$456,114	$22,805	$33,784	$445,135	
72	$445,135	$22,257	$34,460	$432,932	
73	$432,932	$21,646	$35,150	$419,428	
74	$419,428	$20,971	$35,853	$404,547	
75	$404,547	$20,227	$36,570	$388,204	
76	$388,024	$19,410	$37,301	$370,314	
77	$370,314	$18,516	$38,047	$350,782	
78	$350,782	$17,539	$38,808	$329,513	
79	$329,513	$16,475	$39,584	$306,404	
80	$306,404	$15,320	$40,376	$281,348	
81	$281,348	$14,067	$41,184	$254,232	
82	$254,232	$12,711	$42,007	$224,937	
83	$224,937	$11,247	$42,847	$193,336	
84	$193,336	$9,667	$43,704	$159,298	
85	$159,298	$7,965	$44,578	$122,685	
86	$122,685	$6,134	$45,470	$83,349	
87	$83,349	$4,167	$46,379	$41,137	
88	$41,137	$2,058	$47,307	**($4,113)**	

This scorecard indicates that the investor would be able to withdraw an inflation-adjusted $30,000 per year from his portfolio until age 88. As in pre-retirement, this scorecard helps him to monitor his progress and it illustrates whether any adjustments need to be made to the income.

For those who are retired, it is comforting to be able to check your money situation and see how it is doing. That way you can tell if you have a good cushion or if you have to make some adjustments.

Shortfalls

There are only a few ways to reasonably handle any shortfalls in your financial plan. Cutting back may not sound like fun but once you are retired your options are limited. It is the reason I encourage investors to build in a cushion or margin for error.

The pursuit of higher returns

Some investors tend to become more aggressive with their portfolios when they fall behind in their savings goals. They want their investment portfolios to do all the work and if there is a shortfall they will just crank up the risk profile in the hope of a higher return.

A problem occurs when the returns don't come but the risk does. When you are retired, one big market correction can turn a bad situation into a complete disaster. Instead of solving the problem, it only becomes worse.

The worst way to make up for a shortfall in your financial plan is to pursue higher returns by taking risks that are unsuitable. Yet that is what has happened to many investors over the past ten years.

How many financial advisors have said, 'if you just hold on for the long term, the markets will rebound and you will see great returns'? It's one thing if you are 30 years old and have another 35 years of saving in front of you; it is another if you are 60 years old and retirement is looming. It's even worse if you are already retired. The US stock market has shown almost zero gain for the first ten years of this millennium, while the Japanese stock market has been in a state of decline for twenty-five years!

Encouraging investors to be more aggressive by putting more emphasis on stocks is irresponsible and a prolonged bear market can devastate retirees who have little ability to recoup losses. Investors need to determine their tolerance to volatility and find a way to build a portfolio that matches it.

If trying to achieve higher returns is a dangerous gamble in trying to overcome a shortfall, what other options are there?

Realistic solutions

The common denominator is that they *all involve sacrifice* and it is why many people avoid these options.

The solutions available depend upon what stage of life you are at. Someone who is still working has different options than someone who is already retired. In each case, however, those who are proactive about managing their financial situation can take great satisfaction in overcoming any shortfalls.

If you are still saving for retirement, you can increase your contributions to your savings. If you are already retired, you can decrease your withdrawals. It requires some sacrifice and doesn't sound like much fun, but it is better than looking for magical answers or ignoring the situation while risking your future.

Those who are still working could also postpone their retirement for a year or two or longer. There is no equivalent solution for someone who is already retired, unless they can go back to work. Again, it is not an easy choice.

One solution that is becoming more common is the strategy of working part-time in the early years of retirement. It not only supplements income, it provides a transition in lifestyle from being fully employed to being fully retired. There is something to be said for that idea on a lot of levels. Even for those who can afford retirement, staying involved in the workforce can be rewarding in many ways.

Andrew Allentuck's book, 'When Can I Retire?' explores many of the options available to those in retirement, including the option of part-time employment.

While some of these ideas may not seem very appealing, taking a risk in the pursuit of higher returns is an even poorer idea.

Summary

The good news is that if you set some realistic goals, develop an investment plan and stick to investment choices that suit your situation, then the chances are it all should work out. Adjustments to your plan should be minimal and relatively painless.

For some people, it may seem like a lot of work and may sound complicated. They may approach retirement planning by saving what they think they can afford, letting it build up over time and hoping everything works out. The trouble with this approach is that there is always something that seems more important than saving for the future.

Paying yourself first and setting aside 10% of your paycheque for savings is a good idea but it isn't retirement planning. No goals have been set and you have no idea if you are on track or not. Your monthly savings are a tool you can use to help make your plan work, but they are not your plan.

The best strategy is to develop a plan and then measure your performance. That doesn't mean measuring the rate of return on your investments and nothing else; it means checking on your progress to see if you are accumulating enough capital. The more often you check, the more likely it will be that you stay on track.

If you have no interest in these matters, have no time, or have tried it and feel you have no expertise, find a financial advisor who you are comfortable working with. Once you have decided that you have found the right person, tell them what you want to achieve and give them all the information they ask for.

Your chances of success will improve if you take these simple steps.

TRENDS

THE FOLLOWING TRENDS illustrate how serious the problem of lack of saving for the future has become.

A study prepared by the University of Waterloo claims that two-thirds of households appear not to be saving enough to cover basic expenses in 2030.

In 1999 a study prepared by two Statistics Canada analysts, Maser and Dufour, concluded that 33% of the near elderly would not be able to generate total requirement income equivalent to 67% of their working income.

In a study for the Ministry of Finance in the Province of Ontario prepared by Bob Baldwin it was observed in a study by the Chief Actuary (OCA, 2008) that both men and women are working later and later in life. By 2030 it is expected that 14% of women and 25% of men ages 65 to 69 will be engaged in paid work.

Trends in pension plan coverage

Statcan surveys reveal that over the past two decades the percentage of Canadians covered by employer pension plans has fallen. As of 2008 the percentage of the population covered by defined benefit pension plans had dropped to 29% from 38% in 1992. There has been a marked shift away from defined benefit plans and toward defined contribution plans.

The graphs below show the trend in pension plan coverage in Canada:

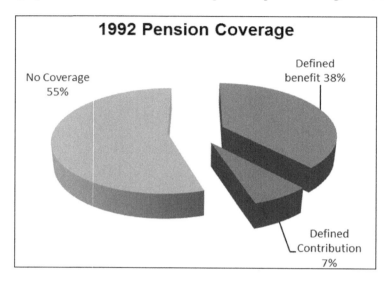

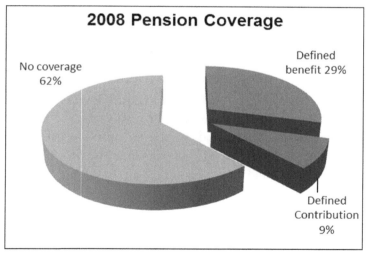

Source: Statistics Canada

In a 2009 study by Bob Baldwin entitled "Research Study on the Canadian Retirement Income System", he concluded that *"In the provincial public and near-public sectors, pension plans have been moving away from the classic DB (defined benefit) structure for nearly 20 years, led by the Ontario Teachers' Pension Plan."*

This trend may be an acknowledgement of the fact that defined benefit plans are far too expensive and create an unacceptable level of cost uncertainty for the plan sponsors.

Trends in Government Benefits

The Canada Pension Plan (CPP) is designed to replace **25% of pre-retirement earnings** up to the yearly maximum pensionable earnings (approximately $51,100 in 2012). Old Age Security (OAS), on the other hand, pays a flat rate rather than a rate based on contributions. As a result, it replaces a higher percentage of pre-retirement income for low income earners and replaces a lower percentage of pre-retirement income for high income earners. Baldwin's study found that OAS, on average, replaced approximately **14% of average pre-retirement income.**

When you combine CPP benefits and OAS benefits, they are designed to replace approximately 35% of pre-retirement income, but that only applies if you continue working until full benefits are payable. Early retirement has a **significant negative impact** on these figures.

Over the past few years our Federal Government has been slowly introducing changes to CPP. As mentioned earlier, those who choose to start drawing their CPP before age 65 face a bigger discount in the benefits they receive. On the other side of the coin, delaying your CPP benefits until later in retirement can significantly increase those benefits.

The maximum CPP benefit in 2012 for those who began withdrawing benefits at age 65 was approximately $1012 per month. CPP benefits are indexed (adjusted upward) to compensate for the effects of inflation.

OAS is also undergoing changes. It was introduced in 1952 to provide income benefits to individuals over the age of 70. The eligibility age was subsequently reduced to 65 and recent legislation will see that increase to age 67 by 2029. Full benefits are provided to individuals with 40 years of residency in Canada, while those with a shorter period of residency will have that benefit reduced. OAS benefits are also indexed to compensate for the effects of inflation.

The maximum OAS benefit in 2012 was approximately $545 per month. For high income earners' OAS benefits, there is a provision where payments begin to be clawed back when your net income reaches approximately $70,000 per year and will be completely clawed back when that income reaches approximately $113,000 per year.

The trend is toward encouraging people to retire later and to rely more and more on their own finances for retirement income.

NOTES:

- Develop your own personal vision for retirement.
- Estimate the income required to satisfy your vision.
- Determine all sources of income available to you in retirement.
- CPP benefits can be reduced by as much as 36% if early retirement is chosen.
- The qualification age for when OAS benefits begin is increasing from age 65 to age 67.
- Inflation has averaged about 2% per year for the past twenty years.
- The rate of return on equities (stock market) has been about 5% per year over inflation for the past fifty years.
- The rate of return on bonds has been about 3% per year over inflation for the past fifty years.
- Investor behaviour has been the biggest single factor contributing to sub-par portfolio performance.
- Use a life expectancy of approximately 90 years of age when planning for retirement.
- Set target values for your portfolio based on what you need to accumulate for retirement and the level of income you will be drawing in retirement.
- Measure your progress on a regular (annual) basis.
- There are two types of employer pension plans; they are defined benefit pension plans and defined contribution pension plans.
- You have to apply to receive your CPP and OAS benefits; payments do not begin automatically.

SECTION FOUR

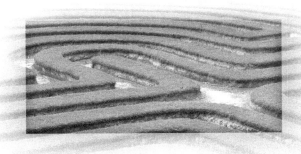

INVESTMENT PLANNING

INTRODUCTION TO INVESTING

Many people believe that the secret to financial success is having the ability to consistently choose the best performing investments for their portfolios. Unfortunately, it is an ability that even the most astute investors in the world do not possess.

The real secret to successful investing is much less exciting; it lays in identifying the mix of investments that suits your needs and having the patience and confidence to stick with it. Two problems can arise. Investors will sometimes stick with investments that don't match their needs or investors will sometimes move out of investments that suit their needs but which have short term under-performance.

In previous sections I have illustrated how you can lay the groundwork by building a vision and a sound plan to achieve that vision. A similar step-by-step approach should be used when choosing your investments and building your portfolio. It requires that you understand the various investments available, how they react to market forces, and how they work together to provide you with the best possible returns given your tolerance to risk.

You owe it to yourself to make informed decisions that are suitable for your unique situation. It is treating your money well.

ASSESSING YOUR TOLERANCE TO RISK

Just as everyone will have a different objective for retirement income, they also have their own unique personality and financial circumstances.

Your personal attributes will help to influence the investment strategy you choose to pursue. They will determine whether you have the personality and financial ability to adopt an aggressive investment strategy that is subject to considerable volatility or whether you should take a more conservative approach.

Your first challenge is to find a way to determine your tolerance to risk and volatility.

Risk and risk tolerance are often discussed when the topic of investing arises but they are seldom defined and even then the definitions vary. Before you can begin an investment plan, you need to know what kind of an investment profile you have.

Assessing your tolerance to risk is the first step you need to take before you make any investment decisions.

Factors to consider

The risk tolerance among individuals will vary based upon their age, experience, net worth, risk capital and even their personality. Each of these elements must be weighed and factored into the final decision. The question becomes how to weigh and factor the elements.

Age

It is generally perceived that a younger investor has a long-term time horizon in terms of the need for investments and can take more risk, while an older individual has a short investment horizon and should take less risk, especially once they have retired.

However, there are a number of other considerations that come into play. Just because you are 65 doesn't necessarily mean that you **must** shift everything to conservative investments.

Investment Objectives

Your investment objectives must be considered when calculating how much risk can be assumed. Are you seeking long term growth; are you seeking income; or are you seeking to protect what you have, even if the possibility of earning a reasonable return is remote? Each of these three simple objectives would require different approaches to investing. It is important to know what you are trying to accomplish.

Investment Experience

Your level of investment experience is an important consideration in determining risk tolerance. Are you relatively new to investing or have you had considerable experience? Do you rely on your advisor for recommendations or do you research your own investments? Have you had experience with a variety of different investments or has it been limited to mutual funds and GICs?

Net worth

Risk capital is money available to invest or trade that will not affect your lifestyle if lost. High net worth investors may have set aside enough capital to ensure a comfortable retirement. If that is the case, the portion of their investments not required to generate retirement income (their risk capital) can be allocated to higher risk investments.

All too often, however, those with low net worth can be drawn to riskier investments because of the lure of large profits that can seemingly be attained quickly and easily. They believe that these investments can be their ticket to financial success that would otherwise be impossible. When the losses mount, the disillusioned investor has fallen even farther behind in his quest for a comfortable retirement.

Personality

While factors such as our age, investment experience and net worth are easy to measure, each of us has our own personality. There are high net worth investors who may be able to afford losses in their portfolios in the pursuit of higher returns but that approach conflicts with their personality. Your personality is a major factor that must be considered along with the more measurable aspects of your investment profile.

KINDS OF RISK

Many investors see risk only in terms of safety of their principal. While that is certainly one risk, there are others; including re-investment risk, inflation risk, and market volatility.

Re-investment risk

Almost no one thinks of a guaranteed investment certificate as having any risk associated with it. After all, the principal is guaranteed, usually up to $100,000 per person. What you don't know is the interest rate you will be able to earn when that GIC matures and you go to re-invest your money.

It is a forgotten risk but over the past twenty-five years investors have been re-investing their GICs at lower and lower rates. Those who assumed rates would remain constant miscalculated badly. Yes, their principal is intact but their financial plan may have fallen behind where they had hoped it would be.

Inflation risk

Inflation slowly erodes the purchasing power of a dollar. Each year costs go up and if your investments are not compensating for that increase you are going backwards. If you go backwards long enough, your investments will no longer generate enough income to satisfy your needs.

The challenge comes in determining how much to compensate for this decrease in purchasing power. Over the past twenty years inflation has averaged just over 2% per year in Canada but it sometimes rears its ugly head at an inopportune time. In the period from 1973 to 1982 the inflation rate in Canada averaged 9.6% per year. A basket of goods that cost $100 at the beginning of that period would have cost over $230 ten years later.

We have been fortunate in Canada during our lifetime. Many countries have experienced hyperinflation when their governments continue to print money in extreme amounts even when there has been no corresponding increase in economic activity. The most notable example is Germany in the 1920s when inflation destroyed their currency and the exchange rate between the mark and the US dollar reached a ratio of **42 trillion to one**! It didn't matter if their principal was safe because it no longer had any value.

That is an extreme example but governments worldwide have been printing excessive amounts of money over the past few years rather than cutting back on government spending. The charge has been led by Ben Bernanke, head of the US Federal Reserve. These policies have increased the risk that inflation could slash the purchasing power of your investments.

Volatility risk

Very few people, if any, have lost all of their money by having it invested in a properly diversified portfolio of stocks and bonds. However, the values will fluctuate up and down, sometimes severely, and it can happen that just when you need your money the most, it is at a low value.

The conundrum is that investors need to accept more volatility in their portfolios to offset re-investment risk and inflation risk. The challenge is to strike an appropriate balance, but before that can be done it is worthwhile to learn more about volatility and how you can expect your portfolio to act.

Understanding volatility

One of the issues that many investors struggle with is their expectations. When they have a financial plan drawn up and one of the underlying assumptions is that their investment portfolio will achieve average annual returns of 6% over the long term, then that is often what they expect... every year.

Nothing could be further from the truth. The last thing an investor should expect is that returns on their portfolio from one year to the next will be even close to the long term average that they are seeking. Over the long term it will tend to average out but on a year-to-year basis it is a roller coaster, particularly in the equity markets.

The roller coaster

From 1900 to 2011 the average annual increase in the Dow Jones Industrial Average, excluding dividends, was about 8% per year. Immediately, that is what many investors expect from the equity portion of their portfolio. Once dividends are factored in and management fees deducted, it seems like a realistic number.

The actual experience is far different. It can be a terrifying roller coaster ride for investors. Even investors who are more realistic can be surprised by short term results. Take, for example, the investor who expects the long term average performance of his equities to be about 8% per year. He considers himself to be knowledgeable and is aware of volatility, expecting his portfolio returns to fall between 4% and 12% per year most of the time. He also realizes that his equities may show significant declines from time to time.

The reality is that the Dow showed gains of between 4% and 12% per year about 12 times in the past 110 years. In the other 98 years, the return was either below 4% or above 12%. In fact, while achieving an average annual gain of about 8% per year, the Dow Jones Industrial Average would have handed investors **losses in over one-third of those years**...so much for expectations!

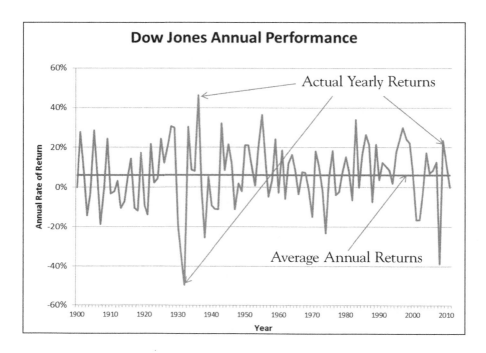

While the *average annual return* (about 8%) is what many investors expect on a yearly basis, that kind of return without volatility exists only in our dreams. It is easy to see that returns are usually significantly higher or significantly lower than the average returns that so many investors expect.

The graph illustrates the actual returns achieved by the Dow Jones Industrial Average in each year since 1900. Few people realize that it is those wildly random returns that, when averaged together, result in that 7% or 8% that we all crave. Two words can be used to describe the returns provided by an investment in the equity markets. They are: inconsistent and unpredictable.

There is one way to almost *completely eliminate volatility* and that is to accept returns on your investment that approach zero. It is not a particularly attractive alternative, especially when you see what inflation does to your purchasing power over time.

Finding the compromise

Can you accept that one out of every three years will generate losses on your portfolio? Can you accept that some of those losses will be greater than 20% or even greater than 30%? That is the history of the Dow Jones Industrial Average and this average includes primarily blue chip companies. Investing in smaller companies or speculative stocks creates even more volatility.

Clearly, there has to be a compromise between taking too much volatility in the pursuit of high returns and accepting zero returns for the sake of eliminating all price fluctuations. Neither of these conditions is acceptable, nor are they likely to help you fulfil your financial objectives.

It is important to consider both emotional and financial factors when determining your ability to tolerate risk. Some individuals may have a personality that enjoys the adrenalin rush of an aggressive investment strategy but that strategy may be inappropriate given their financial circumstances.

Finding your own unique compromise is the key. How much volatility can you accept in your portfolio?

Part of the difficulty is that there is no readily available standard against which investors can measure themselves. What is acceptable and what is excessive? Given that shortcoming, when investors attempt to define that tolerance, many have nothing to rely on but their own intuition. They have an idea that a balance needs to be struck but where should the line be drawn?

While intuition should play a role, we have seen a number of other factors that come into play. Determining the impact of all these factors is a challenge.

ASSESSING YOUR INVESTMENT PROFILE

When completing an account application form, many investors will defer to their financial advisor when trying to determine what their profile might be. In their mind, the advisor has seen numerous investors over the years and therefore should be able to tell them where they fit in the overall scheme of things.

At other times, investors don't attach as much importance to this subject and provide a response without giving it as much thought as they should.

The investment profile provides the blueprint of how a portfolio should be constructed. In other words, it provides the guidelines for an appropriate asset allocation. Doing a good job in this area improves the chances that an investor will be happy with their portfolio.

If you are unsure of where you fit and want a quick way to evaluate your holdings, you can use the following rule of thumb. The total allocation to fixed income should be approximately equal to your age. If you are 60 years old, then approximately 60 percent of your portfolio should be allocated to bonds, if you are a moderate investor. The remainder of the portfolio could be allocated to other asset classes. It's not perfect but it is a reasonable compromise.

Solutions

A better solution is to complete an investment profile questionnaire. The range of questions can vary widely from one to another but they all help to provide investors with somewhat objective guidelines for categorizing themselves.

Some ask questions about how investors might feel if a specific event occurred in the future, how they felt when a specific event occurred in the past or what action they might take should a specific event occur. These are more *emotion based* questionnaires which are very subjective. A more *fact based* questionnaire may be easier to answer accurately.

You can try a couple of different self-evaluation reviews to come up with the most accurate profile possible. If you are working with a financial advisor, most will have access to at least one such questionnaire and possibly more.

Many mutual fund companies also provide risk tolerance questionnaires on their websites. With all of these tools, there is no reason why a diligent investor should not have a reasonable idea of what their investment profile is.

Summary

It is important for you to review your goals and objectives every couple of years. If these goals and tolerance to risk have changed, then so has the ideal asset mix for your portfolios. We all get older every year and even if nothing else changes, that does.

NOTES:

- Factors used in assessing your tolerance to risk include your age, investment objectives, investment experience, net worth and personality.
- Various kinds of risk that can threaten your portfolio can include capital risk, re-investment risk, inflation risk and volatility risk.
- Many investors only consider capital risk.
- Over the past 110 calendar years the stock market in the United States has handed investors negative returns in over one-third of those years.
- Consider using an investment profile questionnaire to assess your tolerance to risk.
- The make-up of your portfolio should reflect the amount of risk you are willing to assume and not the returns you are hoping to achieve.

DIVERSIFICATION AND CORRELATION

Diversification and correlation among asset classes are key concepts when it comes to controlling risk while maintaining the potential to achieve reasonable returns. These may seem like complicated terms but they are simply meant to describe whether your investments complement one another or mimic one another.

Portfolios that lack true diversification are typically more volatile and volatility is a measure of risk.

Many investors understand the concept of diversification but lack the ability to measure it. Others may be aware of the terminology but don't fully grasp what it means when it comes to choosing investments.

In this section, I describe proper portfolio diversification and describe how correlation is used to measure the level of diversification. These are tools used by institutional investors and pension plans. You should use them too.

If, after reading this section, the concepts are somewhat unclear, seek the advice of a financial advisor. But before taking any advice, ensure that the advisor understands the correlation among asset classes and can explain it in simple terms.

First things first

Before you can build a diversified investment portfolio you need to understand the investments that you have to work with. Venturing into the investment world can be like walking into a supermarket without a shopping list. There is so much to choose from. The question is; where to begin?

Just as the grocery shopper needs to choose a variety of foods to create a balanced, healthy diet, investors need variety in their portfolios. A diet of steak and nothing else may be appealing to some but problems would soon emerge. The same applies to an investment portfolio. An unhealthy situation will eventually arise in a portfolio that consists of nothing but equities, for example.

Going back to a balanced diet; the Canada Food Guide has six broad categories or groups of food. These groups include fruits and vegetables, oils and fats, grain, milk, meat and beverages. Each category contributes to the health and well-being of the individual. At the same time, different people require different diets. An infant, a teenager and a retiree will all need something from each group but in different proportions. Within each group, specific choices can be made but each group should be included.

The same approach can be applied to building an investment portfolio. There are several broad categories of investments that are referred to as asset classes. Each asset class should provide a different element to the investment portfolio and contribute to its overall health. It is also important to note that within each asset class there can be good and bad investments.

Investors often jump over the asset allocation process and immediately want to start making individual investment choices. In this situation entire asset classes can be ignored, leading to an unbalanced portfolio that is hazardous to your financial well-being.

Six asset classes

There is a lot of discussion about what the different categories or groups should be but an argument can be made for six separate asset classes or categories. These asset classes include:

- cash
- fixed income
- preferred shares
- equities
- real estate
- precious metals

Some investors may have only one or two asset classes among their investments, while others may have all six. It is important to understand the basic characteristics of each.

Why only six asset classes?

Some publications propose as many as 15 asset classes or more. Within the equity markets, for example, they will separate Canadian equities, US equities and international equities into their own distinct asset classes. I believe it is a false classification.

All companies are trying to earn profits on their operations and grow in value, regardless of whether they operate in Canada, the United States, Europe, Asia or South America. Many Canadian mining companies have significant operations in other countries; should they be classified as Canadian companies or international companies? Separating companies into different asset classes on the basis of where their head office is located doesn't make sense.

Looking at it in another way, ask yourself whether US gold mining giant Newmont Mining is more closely related to Canadian gold mining giant Barrick Gold or to Apple? Newmont and Apple are both US companies, while Newmont and Barrick are both gold mining companies. Yet some would put Newmont Mining in the same asset class as Apple (U.S. equities) but not in the same asset class as Barrick Gold. The truth is that they all belong in the same asset class and that asset class is 'equities'.

Similar classifications are made in the fixed income (bond market) where government bonds, corporate bonds, convertible bonds, foreign bonds and real return bonds are all assigned to different asset classes. While they may have different characteristics, they are all bonds.

The result is too many asset classes which are too much alike.

It is also important to note that within each asset class there can be various sectors with distinct features and characteristics. Equities, for example, can include mining, financial services and technology companies. As mentioned, fixed income can include corporate, real return and convertible bonds. Real estate investment trusts can include office buildings, shopping centres and residential rental properties.

The following charts illustrate the various asset classes and some of the sectors within each.

As you can see, diversification is first achieved at the asset class level and further diversification can then be achieved at the sector level. A well-constructed portfolio will take both levels of diversification into consideration. Individual investments are then made within each sector. Unfortunately, many investors immediately begin choosing individual investments without considering asset classes and sectors.

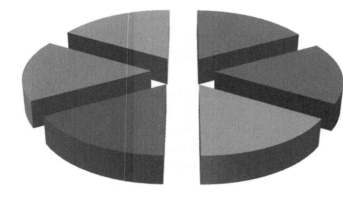

Asset Classes

- Cash
- Fixed Income
- Preferred Shares
- Equities
- REITs
- Precious Metals

Diversification and Correlation

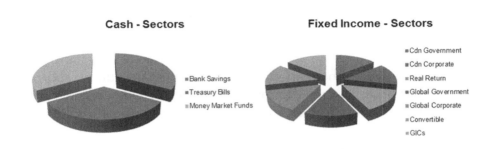

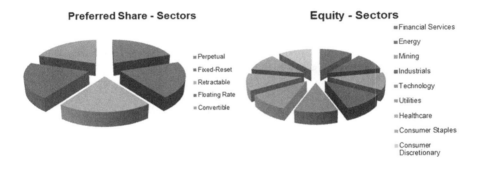

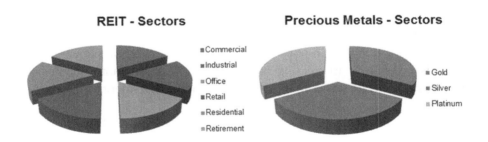

Mutual Funds, Segregated Funds and Exchange Traded Funds

Contrary to what some may believe, mutual funds, segregated funds and exchange traded funds are **not asset classes**. When investors want to participate in a market they can choose an individual investment, such as a particular stock or bond. Alternatively, they can choose to purchase a basket of investments, such as a mutual fund, segregated fund or exchange traded fund (ETF).

If the basket contains nothing but equities, that particular mutual fund would fall into the equity asset class; if it contained nothing but bonds, it would fall into the fixed income asset class. The same applies to segregated funds and exchange traded funds.

These three investment vehicles allow investors to hold a large number of investments all wrapped into a neat package. They will be discussed in more detail later in this section.

What is diversification?

One of the goals of holding a variety of asset classes is to achieve diversification.

When financial advisors talk about diversification they are really talking about how investments or asset classes complement one another. There are times when investors believe they have a diversified portfolio when in reality it is not. A collection of a number of different mutual funds, for example, does not guarantee diversification.

If two investments in a portfolio are acting in exactly the same manner, there is little point in holding both of them. It is far more effective to replace one of the two with an investment that complements the other.

> A hypothetical example would be a portfolio that holds ABC Canadian Equity Mutual Fund and XYZ Canadian Equity Mutual Fund. Generally speaking, they both go up and down with the Canadian stock market. At times one will outperform the other but the difference is negligible. The performance of one **mimics** the performance of the other.

*A second portfolio might hold the same ABC Canadian Equity Mutual Fund as the first but also have an equal amount invested in the ABC Corporate Bond Fund. These two investments act differently to changes in the economic environment and it will be more common for one to show strong performance when the other is struggling. The performance of one **complements** the performance of the other.*

In the first instance the portfolio will lack diversification, while in the second instance diversification is achieved by holding complementary investments.

Definition of correlation

How can you determine whether two investments or assets simply **mimic** one another or whether they **complement** one another? The measurement used to determine the relationship between two investments is known as correlation.

- If two investments move in exactly the same direction, at exactly the same time and at exactly the same rate, their correlation is "1 to 1" (commonly referred to as a correlation of one).

- If two investments move in exactly the opposite direction, at exactly the same time and at exactly the same rate, their correlation is "1 to -1" (commonly referred to as a correlation of minus one).

All correlations fall between plus one and minus one.

Two investments can have a correlation of zero. It simply means that you cannot predict the return on one investment by the return on the other. Sometimes they will move in the same direction and sometimes they will move in opposite directions.

Low correlations and zero correlations indicate proper diversification. Correlations that are skewed to high positive numbers, closer to plus one, result in abnormally volatile portfolios. Correlations that are skewed to high negative numbers, closer to minus one, result in portfolios with lower returns.

The goal is to have a combination of assets that have low correlations to one another. In that way they are more apt to complement one another rather than mimic one another. It doesn't matter whether this low correlation is negative or positive as long as it is low.

It is important to remember that correlation **measures the relationship** between two investments and **not the performance** of those investments. While the correlation between two assets will vary over time, it is still a good tool for trying to minimize volatility. And that is the whole purpose of diversification.

Measurements of Correlation		
	Positive Correlations	Negative Correlations
Low Correlation	0.00 to 0.50	0 to -0.50
Moderate Correlation	0.50 to 0.75	-0.50 to -0.75
High Correlation	0.75 to 1.0	-0.75 to -1.00

Diversification and volatility

It is important to find the middle ground where you get reasonable returns with reasonable volatility from your investment choices. It can seem like advanced math but the principles are relatively simple.

Financial advisors have access to software which illustrates the correlation among a wide variety of different investments. While not every investment can be included in this analysis, a great many can, and this provides the investor with a feel for the level of diversification in their portfolio. It is certainly better than making random investment choices in the hope that they provide diversification.

Canadian equities, US equities and international equities are often classified as separate asset classes but when you look at the correlation numbers, it can be surprising how little value is added by simply adding equities based on the geographic location of their head office is *improper diversification*.

As mentioned earlier, if two investments simply mimic the performance of one another, you don't need both of them. You would be far better off switching one of them to an investment that complements the other. Then you would be far more diversified and your portfolio should have a better risk/return profile.

While that comment may seem repetitive it cannot be stressed enough. Most people measure their portfolio simply by the rate of return it achieves but more are now starting to pay attention to volatility. It is important to include both measures when you are evaluating your portfolio.

Diversification within asset classes

While diversification *among* asset classes is important, so is diversification *within* asset classes. Diversifying between stocks and bonds is one level of diversification but within each of those asset classes you can add another level of diversification. Bank stocks act differently from energy stocks and real return bonds act differently from corporate bonds.

The process is not about trying to guess which will be the best asset class or the best investment within an asset class; it is about ensuring that you have the appropriate allocation among those asset classes and among the various investments within each asset class.

Proper diversification reduces volatility. The problem is that many investors thought they were diversified when they weren't. Correlation helps them to measure that diversification and squeeze out volatility. Of course, the final goal is to maximize returns for the level of risk that is suitable to the client, so it does take a bit of mixing and matching to eventually come up with the ideal asset allocation.

Notes:

- Asset classes are broad categories of investments.
- Six broad categories include cash, fixed income, preferred shares, equities (common shares), real estate and precious metals.
- Sectors are sub-categories that may exist within each asset class.
- Mutual funds, segregated funds and exchange traded funds are not asset classes.
- Diversification refers to investments that complement one another.
- Correlation is a statistic that allows us to measure diversification.
- All correlations fall between -1.0 and +1.0.
- Correlations closer to +1.0 indicate lack of diversification that may result in increased volatility
- Correlations closer to -1.0 indicate over-diversification to the extent that potential returns are diminished.

ASSET CLASSES

IN ORDER TO understand why the value of your portfolio may rise or fall it is important to learn more about the characteristics of investments within each asset class. And a better understanding can lead to better decisions regarding your investment choices.

The various asset classes were suggested because they tend to complement one another. Individual investments should be chosen on the same basis. In other words, the correlation among individual investments should also be low.

Of course, it would be ideal if the best performing individual investment could be chosen year after year, but that is an unrealistic expectation that is unlikely to be fulfilled. A better course of action is to pick good solid investments that tend to complement each other as much as possible in each asset class.

The choices don't even have to be the best ones in each asset class; they simply need to be reasonable choices made with sound logic. In some asset classes, such as gold and cash, there isn't much opportunity for choice. In others, like equity and fixed income, the options are almost unlimited.

Given the six asset classes and the various choices within each, investors may be left a bit confused as to which individual investments fall within each asset class, the characteristics of those investments and the factors that affect their value and, ultimately, their performance.

Inconsistency

The problem with every asset class is that the returns are not consistent from one year to the next.

While the historical long term rates of return for various asset classes can be determined, and the average rate of return is a convenient number to work with, it paints a completely inaccurate picture of what investors can expect.

When the stock market is down 30% one year, up 40% the next year and followed by a 20 % return in the third year, the average return is about 5.5% per year but it doesn't feel like it. Nothing close to 5.5% has been achieved in any of those years, yet when an investor sees an average long term rate of return of 5.5%, that is what they expect, every year.

Since 1900 the US stock market, as measured by the Dow Jones Industrial Average, has posted negative returns in approximately one third of the calendar years. Generally speaking, any time you make an investment in the stock market you have a 33% chance of losing money over the subsequent twelve months. Returns on individual stocks are even less predictable. Despite that, the equity markets have provided positive returns over the long term.

The same inconsistencies apply to other asset classes in varying degrees.

In order to understand why these wild swings occur, it is important to understand the factors that affect the valuations of various investments. Understanding these factors can also help investors make decisions within their portfolios that can help improve the consistency of returns from one year to the next.

CASH

CASH HAS BECOME a forgotten asset class, but it wasn't a forgotten asset class in the 1980s when yields on money market investments reached over 15%. In 2011 Money Sense published a magazine entitled 'Guide to the Perfect Portfolio' that took asset classes to a whole new level. It identified fifteen different asset classes, including six different classes of equities and five different classes of bonds.

If the goal is to make the choices more complicated, then suggesting fifteen asset classes, many with similar characteristics, will likely do the trick. Yet cash was not included among the asset classes even though it provides completely different characteristics from any of the fifteen listed.

Cash includes highly liquid investments such as the balances in your savings accounts, money market funds, treasury bills or bonds maturing in less than one year. It is money you can access and spend on short notice, usually without fees or penalties for withdrawal.

It is easy to scoff at cash as an investment when rates are low but it isn't always that way. Just because an investment is out of favor doesn't mean it shouldn't be included as an asset class. Every asset class will have periods where it may be the best performing investment or the worst.

Two characteristics of cash are its price stability and its liquidity. Investors can be relatively certain of what the value of their cash investments will be if they need to access them and they know they can access that cash very quickly and easily.

In normal conditions cash carries a lower interest rate than longer term fixed income investments and in normal conditions the rate of return on cash investments should be higher than the rate of inflation. In recent years central banks around the world have artificially lowered short term rates to levels below the rate of inflation.

When short term rates are higher than long term rates, yields are said to be inverted and this can often be the precursor to an economic recession. Economic recessions can lead to stock market corrections and a decline in equity values. In these circumstances cash becomes an important asset class and should not be overlooked.

When short term rates are lower than inflation, a different problem is created. The purchasing power of an investor's cash will become less and less as time goes on. This deterioration in purchasing power can lead some investors to deploy a portion of their cash in other asset classes. In the past gold has often been a beneficiary when this situation occurs.

A quick glance at rates on treasury bills or a six month GIC, for example, should reveal a rate that is higher than inflation but lower than long term rates. If this is not the case, something is amiss.

Perhaps the best choice for cash in a portfolio is government treasury bills. They are extremely safe and highly liquid, meaning that cash is available on short notice. Unfortunately, the minimum amount available for investment is sometimes beyond the average investor. A compromise may be a money market mutual fund.

Short term GICs (with less than one year to maturity) are less appealing because they lack the liquidity of a treasury bill. Cashable GICs are somewhat better but may carry a slightly lower rate than a short term GIC.

The asset allocation exercise will indicate, more or less, how much of the portfolio should be apportioned to cash. Tactical considerations, such as an inverted yield situation, may imply a slight variation from the proposed asset allocation. From there, the investor can decide which of the various cash investments best suits their needs.

Cash valuations

Cash may be the most stable of all the asset classes - the principal value rarely fluctuates. The rates of return vary far less than other assets and that rate is primarily linked to inflation. If inflation rises, so does the interest rate on cash investments.

From time to time, governments and central banks in their wisdom try to push the interest rate on cash below the rate of inflation. That means your cash will buy less in the future than it will buy today, even when you add in the interest it may have earned. It is done in an effort to get people to spend their money and stimulate the economy. Many economists will tell you that it doesn't work; many others will tell you that it does.

The yield on cash and other short term investments relative to the yield on longer term bonds is an indicator that is watched by many market strategists and economists. When the yield on cash is higher than on ten year bonds, for example, there is a good chance that an economic recession is right around the corner. It is not a guarantee that a recession will occur but it happens with disturbing regularity.

In the past, recessions have led to a period of sub-par stock market performance. All of this is related to an inventory cycle where a build-up of inventory and low sales affect corporate profits.

The following charts are examples of how short term rates compare to long term rates in a normal interest rate environment and in an inverted interest rate environment.

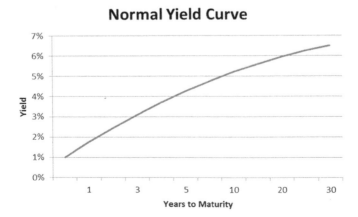

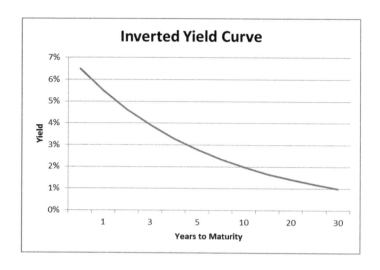

FIXED INCOME

FIXED INCOME IS an asset class that is misunderstood by a great many investors and it is worth spending some time learning more about it.

Regardless of the issuer, all fixed income investments pay an interest rate and repay the principal at a pre-determined maturity date. The interest payments are a contractual obligation, as is the repayment of the principal. Fixed income investments include bonds (or debentures) and GICs. Bonds can be issued by governments and corporations, both domestic and foreign. Each will have slightly different characteristics from the others.

In the case of corporate bonds, interest payments are made from pre-tax income, while government bonds are paid from tax revenues, but they are all bonds.

Since all fixed income investments carry the same two major characteristics, an interest rate and a maturity date, they belong in the same asset class. Some of the secondary characteristics of a bond can include an inflation adjustment component, the opportunity to convert the bonds into common shares, or a variety of other characteristics.

Some firms and publications have advocated different asset classes for the purpose of recognizing the unique features that a bond may offer. However, splitting fixed income investments into several different asset classes doesn't change these two major characteristics. If the decision is to split fixed income investments into completely separate asset classes because of a unique feature, then it would be difficult to stop at five.

Challenges in the bond market

Despite rarely making the headlines in the financial media, the bond market is significantly larger than its more glamorous partner…the stock market. This is partially due to the fact that governments issue bonds when they need to borrow money; they don't issue stocks, and the government bond market is enormous.

With the size of the bond market, it seems like it should be relatively easy to find the appropriate selections for a portfolio. That isn't always the case. Pension plans, mutual funds and other institutional investors will often swoop in and pick up large quantities of the best bonds. Banks will also get in on the action. They might pay a nominal interest rate to a customer on a savings account and use the proceeds to buy a higher yielding bond. They can earn a tidy profit by capturing the 'spread' between the two interest rates.

So the average investor has lots of competition when it comes to buying bonds.

There are other challenges when it comes to buying bonds. There is no central market as there is with the stock market, so even trying to find what is available can be a challenge. There are also other administrative factors to consider, such as re-investing interest payments and finding new bonds to replace those that are maturing in a portfolio.

Unlike stocks, bonds have a maturity date and the profile of a bond portfolio changes over time if no action is taken. Over time, a ten-year bond will become a five-year bond, a two-year bond and eventually cash. In order to ensure that a bond portfolio has a relatively constant profile it must be actively managed.

An investor can buy and hold a stock literally forever. The same cannot be said for a bond because it will mature.

Fixed Income

A Closer Look

On the surface, bonds and GICs may seem simple to understand. They pay an interest rate and they have a maturity date; it is a simple concept to grasp. It provides a level of comfort. But there are valid reasons to scrutinize the fixed income market more closely.

In a rising interest rate environment short term bonds perform better than long term bonds; in falling interest rate environments the reverse is true. At times corporate bonds perform better than government bonds, while at other times government bonds are the better investment. What are the implications of buying a bond at a premium or a discount? How do real returns bonds perform in various market conditions? How can credit quality be checked and what credit quality is appropriate? When should GICs be used rather than bonds as a fixed income investment in a portfolio?

Investors will often focus on the maturity date. They know what the yield on a specific bond will be over that time but once that bond matures, they have no idea what the opportunities will be going forward.

In addition, if more than one bond is held in a portfolio, an overall yield to maturity for the portfolio cannot be calculated. For example, if an investor holds a 3-year bond or GIC in their portfolio and a 5-year bond in their portfolio, they cannot calculate what the return will be for the next 5 years because the bond that matures in 3 years will have to be re-invested and no one knows what the rate will be.

The tendency is for investors to consider each bond individually and somehow extrapolate that in a yield to maturity. With several different maturity dates and several different yields to maturity, that calculation is impossible. The current yield on each bond, however, **can** be calculated in the same way it can be calculated on a bond mutual fund or a bond ETF (exchange traded fund).

Once an investor holds more than one bond in their portfolio, it is akin to holding a bond mutual fund or a bond ETF. In the first case, the investor makes the choices for the individual bond investments and in the second case the manager of the mutual fund or ETF makes the choices. In both cases, a portfolio of bonds holds each with varying maturities, interest rates and other features.

If you could take a can opener and open up the portfolio of a bond mutual fund, the yield to maturity of every bond in that portfolio could be calculated and listed on a spreadsheet. In fact, for those who want to take the time to glean through an annual report, it could be done...not in a timely fashion, but it could be done.

Bond mutual funds and bond ETFs do provide statistical information on the bonds in their portfolios. The current yield of the bonds, the average duration and the credit quality of the bonds is released on a regular basis. The name of the actual issuer of each bond in the portfolio is also listed.

For the core holdings of a fixed income portfolio a mutual fund or ETF can help to reduce the administrative chores, eliminate the task of choosing which of the many individual bonds are appropriate and provide instant diversification across issuers, maturity dates and credit quality. That doesn't mean there aren't excellent opportunities among individual bonds because there are. Investors have to decide for themselves which approach works best or if a combination of mutual funds, ETFs and individual bonds is the most appropriate.

Sticking to GICs has its drawbacks; the major one is lack of liquidity. When an investor chooses a five year GIC, for example, that money is inaccessible for five years. If an emergency arises, if the investor's goals change, if the investor decides to make a major purchase or if a better opportunity arises, the money invested in that GIC is not available. This restrictive feature should not be overlooked or underestimated.

On the other side of the coin, most GICs carry a guarantee of principal and interest subject to certain limitations. If an investor does choose a GIC, it is important to be aware of the terms of the guarantee.

All of this illustrates the complexities of the bond market. It can be very rewarding and, managed properly, it becomes an important part of an investment portfolio. A financial advisor can help walk investors through all the options and provide them with some direction when making those difficult decisions.

Fixed Income Valuations

Like cash, bonds are affected by inflation. Because the investor has 'lent' their money to the bond issuer for a longer period of time, there is a greater risk that something unforeseen could happen to the issuer, making repayment difficult. As a result, the investor typically demands and gets a higher rate of return on longer term bonds.

Here is where bonds get tricky and where the misunderstanding often occurs among retail investors with regard to the rate of return on their bonds.

> We can take the hypothetical example of an investor who buys a $10,000 fifteen year bond that has a coupon of 5%. All else being equal, the investor will collect his interest on a regular basis and the principal will be paid at maturity, in fifteen years. It is at the point in time when the issuer redeems the bond, not before and not later.

But interest rates never remain constant and over a fifteen year period there are likely to be periods when interest rates are high and periods when they are low. However, this hypothetical investor has purchased a bond that will pay $500 interest year after year. But the investor may want to sell his bond before it matures.

> Should prevailing interest rates rise to 7% and the investor want to sell his bond prior to maturity, there wouldn't be a lot of interested buyers. After all, why take $500 per year when you can go elsewhere and get $700 per year ($10,000 x 7%)? In order to make his bond attractive to buyers, the investor would have to sell it at a discount and that discount would be of sufficient size that the total return to maturity would be 7%.
>
> Conversely, if interest rates had dropped to 3%, the investor would have buyers clamoring for his bond. But why would an investor give away a 5% bond when everything else was paying only 3%? The short answer is they wouldn't. In this case, the investor who bought the bond could command a premium price for his bond.

The chart below illustrates how the price of a bond changes with interest rates. In this example the bond was purchased at $100 with a 5% annual yield and term to maturity of fifteen years. As interest rates fluctuated between 3% and 7%, the value at which the investor could sell the bond would also fluctuate. In the end it would mature at $100 and the investor would have collected 30 semi-annual interest payments of $2.50 each for a total of $75 along with the original $100.

You will notice that fifteen years prior to maturity a change in current interest rates has a far greater impact on bond prices than it does two or three years prior to maturity.

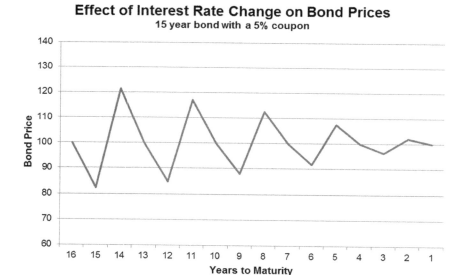

The market price of a bond listed on a client statement reflects the price of that bond if it is sold prior to maturity. It does not reflect the price at maturity. Any bond sold prior to maturity runs the risk of being sold below its purchase value. There is also an opportunity for the sale of the bond at a premium at some point. The longer the term of the bond, the greater the chance of one of those situations arising.

The principal value of a bond mutual fund will fluctuate with interest rate changes in much the same way as the principal value of an individual bond fluctuates.

As you can see, the value of a long term bond will fluctuate in value much more than a short term bond but mutual funds are different. When you first buy a long term bond it can be very volatile in price but that volatility will fall as the bond approaches maturity.

Bond mutual funds will act somewhat differently. The managers usually keep the duration in a pre-determined range. Long duration funds will always hold bonds with longer terms to maturity, and conversely, short duration funds will hold short term bonds. Because the duration remains relatively constant over time, the potential volatility of a bond fund will also remain relatively constant and won't decrease over time.

An investor who expects interest rates to rise would hold shorter term bonds, while the investor who expects rates to fall would hold longer term bonds. The bond calculators at www.moneypages.ca allow you to calculate the impact of interest rate changes on the value of your bond portfolio.

Keep in mind that this change in value represents the change in the principal value of the bond and not in the interest it pays. A bond can fall in value but given a high enough interest rate, it can still provide a positive return. The principal value of a bond can also rise and when added to the interest earned, it can provide a return in excess of the coupon (interest) rate.

If you purchase a long term bond, its value could swing substantially prior to maturity but as it nears maturity, the price becomes more and more stable, eventually maturing at its face value. At any point before maturity, however, the price of the bond could be above its face value or below its face value depending upon the interest (coupon rate) rate of the bond and the current interest rates.

Of course, when valuing bonds and anticipating how they might perform going forward, other features and characteristics of the bonds need to be considered. Do they have a high coupon rate or a low coupon rate? Are they trading at a premium or a discount? What is the credit quality of the bond? Do they have a step-up feature? Are they a fixed-rate bond or an inflation adjusted bond? Are they convertible?

One of the most disconcerting things that can happen to an inexperienced investor is to see the market value of their bond portfolio dropping. It seems incomprehensible that a supposedly safe investment could drop in value but it happens frequently as interest rates fluctuate.

A common reaction to the movement in bond prices can be a retreat by some investors back into GICs. Each statement comfortably lists the purchase price of the GIC without any price swing. Of course, the price is an illusion because it does not reflect the price an investor would realize if they tried to sell the GIC prior to maturity.

A GIC is a non-marketable investment. The institution which issued the GIC will not redeem the GIC prior to maturity except in the most extreme cases and often with a penalty, regardless of whether interest rates have moved in favor of the investor or not. Bluntly put, many investors are deluded into thinking that their GIC portfolios have more price stability than a similar bond portfolio. It simply appears that way because the actual price that an investor could receive on a GIC prior to maturity is not published.

The fixed income space can be very rewarding but it involves more than shopping for the best rate on GICs. It is an area where a financial advisor can provide some meaningful guidance and a good fund manager can add value.

PREFERRED SHARES

I F CASH IS the forgotten asset class then preferred shares are an unknown asset class to many. Investors sometimes think of preferred shares as a variation on common shares or stock. While common shares represent ownership in a company, preferred shares do not. In fact, preferred shares are more like the distant cousin of bonds, rather than common shares, and they pay a dividend, usually on a quarterly basis.

Part of the confusion surrounding preferred shares is in the name because both preferred shares and common shares are called shares. The other similarity comes in the form of distributions made. Preferred shares pay dividends and the distributions made to common shareholders are also dividends.

However, preferred shares are a contractual obligation made by the company issuing them. While companies have one series of common shares (in rare cases, two series), there can be several different series of preferred shares issued by the same company. The terms of the contractual obligation will differ from one series of preferred shares to another and these terms can include the term maturity of the preferred share, the dividend rate, a dividend adjustment provision, a share buyback provision and so on.

These contractual obligations of a preferred share very closely resemble the contractual obligations of a bond. Unlike common shares where dividends are declared and paid at the discretion of the board of directors, the dividends of preferred shares are a contractual obligation. In other words, while the board of directors of a company can choose to reduce or suspend the dividend of their common shares, they must pay the dividend of a preferred share.

One of the main differences between a preferred share and a bond is in the form of the distribution. The former pays a dividend and the latter pays interest. Dividends are paid after the company has paid tax on its earnings and interest is paid before the company pays tax on its earnings. It is an important differentiation because, in an effort to avoid double taxation on the same earnings, dividends are taxed at a lower rate in taxable investment accounts.

There is no advantage to dividends in tax sheltered accounts such as RRSPs and TFSAs. It is also important to note that only dividends of Canadian companies receive preferential tax treatment. Dividends of US companies and other international companies are taxed at the same level as interest.

Another important difference is the safety of investments. In the event of a company bankruptcy the assets can be sold to pay the obligations. Standing at the front of the line are the bankers who have loaned money to the company; next in line are the bond holders, followed by the preferred shareholders. If there is any money left over once these contractual obligations are satisfied, it will be divided among the common shareholders.

The term 'contractual obligation' appears again. There is an obligation to repay the preferred shareholders, but there is no obligation to repay the common shareholders. If they want to participate in the potential growth of the company where bond holders and preferred shareholders do not, then they must stand at the back of the line when things go wrong. The common shareholders take more risk for the potential reward.

Since preferred shares do not represent any ownership in the company, they do not benefit as the company grows in value, nor do they typically suffer to the same extent if the company falls in value. As such, the opportunity for capital gain or loss is more limited with preferred shares than common shares. In a word, they are less volatile.

Because preferred shares pay dividends rather than interest and because they are at a different level in the hierarchy of the corporate structure of a company, they deserve to be in their own asset class.

Compared to the world equity markets and the bond markets, the preferred share market is tiny...miniscule, in fact. But that doesn't mean it isn't an important asset class and it shouldn't be overlooked. Preferred shares are particularly relevant in taxable investment accounts where the dividend tax credit provides an advantage for dividends over interest.

Preferred shares have a lot of characteristics that make them similar to bonds. Where bonds have a contractual obligation to pay interest, preferred shares have a contractual obligation to pay a dividend. The dividend policy on common shares is at the discretion of the company and they can remain the same, be increased, decreased or eliminated at any time.

Valuations

When selecting preferred shares for a portfolio, the analysis can be very similar to analyzing a bond investment. The quality of the issuer, the dividend yield and other factors must all be considered. Some preferred shares have a maturity date, some have fixed dividends, some have floating rate dividends, some are known as perpetual preferreds with redemption features and some are re-set preferreds where the dividend yield can be adjusted on a specific date.

All of these features can be intimidating for the novice investor. However, for those who are willing to do a little extra work, the rewards can be significant. A financial advisor can help investors walk through the myriad of features that may or may not make a specific preferred share a sound investment at any point in time.

In spite of those challenges, it is not an asset class that should be overlooked, but careful selection of the individual securities is essential. Diversification by investment features, by issuer, by industry and so on, are important considerations.

Preferred shares often **react to interest rate changes in a similar manner to bonds,** depending on some of the unique features the preferred share may have. They can also carry other unique features. Some are perpetual preferreds, some are fixed-rate reset preferreds and some are floating rate preferreds. And like bonds, the credit quality of preferred shares can vary.

Because preferred shares may not be easily accessible to some investors, this asset class is sometimes included within the fixed income asset class. Using that approach, there would be five asset classes to consider for inclusion in a portfolio.

EQUITIES

Equities are the rock stars of the investment world. They are glamorous, volatile and get all of the attention. They can be very good or very bad; they are loved, hated and feared. Some television channels are devoted almost entirely to the stock markets and their machinations.

With all of the hype it is easy for investors to lose perspective. In the media every opportunity seems to be better than the last and portfolios often drift towards equities at the expense of other asset classes. The biggest struggle is to have the discipline to keep emotion out of your investment decisions. It is easy to become too enthusiastic or too apprehensive about investing in equities.

Stock market valuations are subject to more comment and more scrutiny than any other asset class. Individual stocks and the indexes themselves are the primary topic of conversation on high powered financial channels such as CNBC, MSNBC and BNN. Books like 'The Intelligent Investor" by Benjamin Graham, "Bull's Eye Investing" by John Mauldin and "One Up on Wall Street" by Peter Lynch outline their approaches to investing in stocks and the stock market and are worth reading.

Equities represent ownership (or at least partial ownership) of a company. Investors share in the growth in value of a company through the growth in value of their shares(s) of the company. If a company declines in value, the value of the investors' share of the company also declines.

The equity asset class includes many different sectors, including energy, mining, financial services, manufacturing, utilities, health care, technology and so on. Each of these sectors will react differently to economic influences and shrewd investors will ensure they have appropriate exposure to the various sectors.

The manufacturing sector, for example, will often react in a positive manner to lower oil prices, while the energy sector will not. Ensure that you have appropriate diversification or ask your advisor for assistance in this area.

The two ways in which equities provide a return to investors are the dividends they pay and the change (hopefully growth) in the value of their shares. Depending upon the prevailing circumstances, far more emphasis is often placed on one rather than the other, but both provide an important contribution to the total return achieved by the investor.

Valuations

One of the biggest challenges faced by investors is determining the fair value of the equity market and the outlook for its value in the future. When compared to the asset classes of cash, fixed income and preferred shares, there are more factors affecting equity values and they are more difficult to measure. Two of these factors are earnings and investor expectations.

Because the equity market is simply a collection of individual companies, the principles that apply to the market also apply to individual companies. When examining equity valuations, the terms will be used interchangeably.

Fundamental Analysis - Earnings

Earnings drive a company's (or the market's) value. They are necessary to enable a company to pay dividends and earnings are necessary for a company to expand and grow. The greater the earnings, the more value a company will be. It is the most basic principle of investing in equities.

Factors that can affect a company's earnings are the level of sales they achieve, the profit margin on their sales, the interest the company must pay on money it has borrowed and so on. In periods of economic strength sales and margins are expected to grow, while in recessions, sales and margins are expected to decline.

It is not only the current level of earnings that determines the value of equities; it is the level of earnings they are expected to achieve in the future. If investors expect that a company's earnings will rise, they will often pay a premium over fair value in the expectation that rising earnings will result in an increased fair value.

Fair value of a company (or the equity market) is often measured by its price earnings ratio.

Price Earnings Ratio

Over time the average value of publicly traded companies has been about 16 times its annual earnings with the value falling between 10 and 20 times its annual earnings the majority of the time. This ratio between the earnings per share of a company and its share price is known as its price-earnings ratio or PE ratio.

Outside those parameters the markets could be considered cheap or expensive but as the previous chart shows, the price of stocks or the value of the overall markets can stay cheap or expensive for much longer than we expect. As you can see, markets can go from overvalued to more overvalued, but eventually **values revert to the mean**. In other words, the market eventually reverts to a value that is close to the long term average multiple of its earnings.

The chart below illustrates the average value of companies traded on the US stock market compared to their earnings per share.

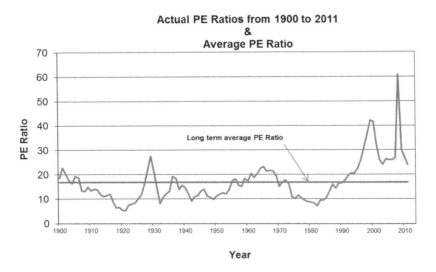

Another way of looking at this chart would be to say it illustrates the share value of a company that earns $1 per share. It is also important to remember that the market doesn't necessarily have to drop to bring valuations back into line. An increase in earnings could accomplish the same thing.

Investor Expectations

While PE ratios are a *good measure of value,* they are a poor statistic to use when trying to time the purchase or sale of an investment. As the chart indicates, they can go from slightly overvalued to being significantly overvalued before coming back to fair valuation levels.

What, then, makes a company that earns $1 per share worth $10 at one point in time (year 1980 on the chart above) and worth $40 at another point in time (year 2000 on the chart)? If the earnings are at the same level, should the price not be at the same level?

It is obvious that other factors influence price and one of these is investor expectations.

The problem with PE ratios is that they are a snapshot in time that measures current price against current earnings. Investments, however, are made with an eye to the future. When someone expects earnings to rise, they will often pay a premium over the historical price earnings ratio.

Let's look at a hypothetical example.

> *An investor looks at a company that has $1 in earnings per share. Using the historical average PE ratio, the fair value would be about $16 per share but it is trading at $24 or a PE ratio of 24. However, this investor believes that earnings will reach $2 per share next year and with a PE ratio of 16, the fair price would be $32. At $24 these shares seem to be a bargain. In this case, the investor's expectations play a big part in the price of the stock.*

Technical Analysis - Charts

While fundamental analysis examines such factors as earnings, book values, interest coverage and so on, technical analysis involves examining charts of the price movements on the markets and stocks. The theory is that price movements reflect investor expectations and technical analysts attempt to draw conclusions from the way in which the price of the market moves.

You will hear terms such as technical support or technical resistance which represents the values at which the equity market will have some support from falling further or resistance to rising higher.

Sometimes a picture is worth a thousand words. A quick glance at a chart can easily tell you if a stock has been going up, down or sideways over any given time frame. That movement has been examined in a thousand different ways by a thousand different technical analysts each trying to draw conclusions about the future from what they see.

There have been hundreds of books written about technical analysis, each having claimed to uncover the secret indicators that can make you rich. A dose of skepticism is appropriate here but that does not mean that chart analysis is not worthwhile. Used in conjunction with fundamental analysis, these charts can be helpful in painting a clearer picture of the situation.

I will look at one technical indicator, the moving average price, and leave it to you to decide if you want to pursue the topic further.

Moving average price

The 200 day moving average price is the average price at which the market (or an individual stock) traded over the previous 200 business days. Because it averages out all the highs and lows over the previous 200 days, it is much less volatile than the day-to-day price. As such it can provide a clearer picture of what long term value investors place on the stock or the index.

If the 200 day moving average reflects the fair price over a long term it becomes a useful comparison to the current market price. If the price is 20% above its 200 day moving average price, it may have got ahead of itself and if it is 20% below its 200 day moving average it may be undervalued. If prices 'revert to the mean', the chances are that an overvalued market will eventually drop and an undervalued market will eventually rise. Using this method to monitor price movements can be applied to individual stocks as well as the overall market.

The TMX Group has an excellent website (www.tmx.com) where you can create your own customized charts. The following example is a ten year chart of BCE along with its 200 day moving average price.

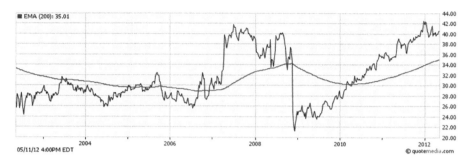

Source: www.tmx.com

Investors wanting to jump into the market might want to wait if the market is over-valued while those who are on the verge of panic and want to sell might want to wait if the market is under-valued. These are not precise timing mechanisms but they can give investors a feel for the value of the market or an individual equity relative to its historic price.

Dividends – A Major Consideration

Many investors focus on the change in share price of an equity investment without considering dividends. When you invest in a company that pays no dividends, you are relying solely on growth in share value to generate a return on your investment. On the other hand, when you invest in a company that pays dividends, those dividends can generate a significant portion of the return and you are not a reliant on growth in share value.

A *word of caution* should be raised about dividend paying investments. In times of low interest rates and uncertain stock markets, investors will often seek out yields in other areas. Stocks that pay high dividends can become the focus of their attention and as a result, they may be tempted to overpay for these stocks. For example, an investor may be tempted to pay more than 16x earnings for a company that pays a high dividend. Use caution when paying a high price-earnings multiple for a dividend paying stock.

In an effort to attract investors, companies can sometimes pay a higher dividend than they can really afford, leaving little money available to operate and grow the company. The dividend payout ratio is the amount paid out in dividends relative to the earnings of the company. A dividend payout ratio in excess of 100% is obviously a very bad sign.

Dividend payout ratios are a more useful tool when used for selecting individual stocks than for choosing a mutual fund or exchange traded fund.

Equity traps to avoid

Hundreds of books have been written about uncovering value in the stock market. Some of the most famous of these have been written by Benjamin Graham, including "The Intelligent Investor" which was first published in 1949.

Rather than repeating what has already been written by others and pointing out all of the ways in which equities can be valued, it might be more useful to highlight a couple of traps to avoid.

Familiarity trap

When an individual works for a company or when a company has a significant presence in a community there can often be a tendency to develop a bias towards that company. Investors shouldn't **confuse familiarity with safety**. If the company seems sound and it fits within the investor's profile then a reasonable allocation may be appropriate.

Past performance trap

Using past performance to guide future expectations is common among mutual fund investors. Economic conditions change, governments change, technology advances, wars erupt and the supplies of food and energy are disrupted. In the environment of those constantly changing circumstances it is irrational to expect the future to look like the past. Yet that expectation constantly repeats itself.

Rather than looking to what the future may hold and ways in which to take advantage of the changes, many investors are more interested in the past performance of a mutual fund investment. While that can provide some insight into the manager's effectiveness compared to that of his peers, it provides absolutely no insight into what future performance may be.

Using past performance as the basis for making your investment decisions is like driving down a freeway looking only in your review mirror. It may work out, but it wouldn't be because it was a good idea.

Summary

Whether you are using fundamental or technical analysis to make your investment decisions, the experience can be frustrating because the markets don't cooperate as often as we would like them to. Equities, including individual stocks or a basket like mutual funds, can go from being overvalued to even more overvalued. You might also buy them when they seem undervalued in the hope of a quick gain, only to find the price drops even further.

These kinds of price movements seem irrational and they are, but it is important to keep in mind that the markets can stay irrational for much longer than we expect.

A company's fortunes do not change minute by minute, hour by hour, day after day. Big changes occur over time, yet the price can fluctuate wildly on a daily basis. Obviously, these constant price changes are not always the result of structural changes within the company.

It is the expectation of what a stock will do in the future that influences whether the investor buys or sells today. If expectations drop, buyers will be scarce and those who want to sell may have to lower their price. Conversely, improving expectations will find a multitude of buyers, and sellers may increase their asking price.

Expecting to predict short term price movements is akin to having the ability to read the minds and emotions of millions of investors instantaneously. In the long run, the price of a stock or an index will reflect their underlying fundamentals, but in the short term expectations and emotion can cause big swings in price.

REITS
(REAL ESTATE INVESTMENT TRUSTS)

NOT EVERYONE CAN afford to buy a rental property with the goals of collecting a monthly cheque and having the property rise in value over time. Even those who can afford it and think it is a good idea may not want to become involved in the day-to-day details of maintenance, collecting cheques and making certain that insurance coverage is in place.

A second approach by those who are attracted to the real estate market is flipping houses. An investor will buy a property that they feel is undervalued, make some improvements and then attempt to sell the property for a profit. It can be rewarding but it might be more accurately considered an active business venture rather than a passive investment.

Knowledge of the local real estate market is only one factor. How will the project be financed? What are the real estate fees and legal fees? What permits will be required? Who makes the improvements? Is it something you can do yourself or will contractors be required? What will the costs be and when will the project be completed? It can become complicated very quickly but there is still a simple way for you to participate in the real estate market.

Real estate investment trusts, or REITs, are unique business structures that provide investors with access to a wide variety of real estate markets. Some REITs own office towers, others own shopping centres, apartment buildings and so on. Still others are diversified among several different types of real estate holdings. Most pay a tax advantaged distribution similar to a dividend.

Generally speaking, the income generated from leases is distributed to the investors after such expenses as mortgage payments on the properties, property management fees, maintenance and so on. In many cases the tenants are signed to long term lease agreements where payments increase over time.

The units of publicly traded REITs can be bought or sold on the world's various stock exchanges including the TSX in Canada. Despite the fact that the real estate market is very large, there were no REITs included in the S&P/TSX Composite Index in Canada as of the end of the 2012 calendar year. When the stock market summary appears in the financial media every day, the value of the various REITs in Canada is not reflected in that summary.

Investors who bought an index mutual fund that replicated the TSX index had no exposure to REITs. What were they missing? Quite a bit, actually. In 2012, REITs provided better performance than the broad equity market and did so with much less volatility. In fact, the volatility of the REIT market in Canada has been consistently less volatile than the S&P/TSX index for a number of years.

Research by Ibbotson Associates (source www.reit.com) on the REIT sector in the United States found that:

- An investment in REITs has historically increased the total return to an investor with a balanced portfolio.

- An investment in REITs has complemented an investment in equities and bonds by reducing risk or volatility over time.

- Growth in the distributions paid by REITs has outpaced inflation for the past ten years (2010).

REIT Valuations

Many of the factors that affect the equity markets, such as earnings per share and investor expectations, also affect the value of real estate investment trusts and, as with equities, technical analysis can be used to examine their price movements.

The earnings of REIT shares are determined in large part by the stream of rental revenue. That revenue stream, in turn, can be affected by interest rates paid on mortgage and the rental rates. Occupancy rates are another concern.

Mortgage rates

Most of the properties held by a REIT have a mortgage and higher interest rates mean higher mortgage payments, thus reducing the stream of revenue available for distribution to investors.

Rental rates

The level of rents is usually determined by supply and demand but in many commercial buildings tenants sign long term lease contracts. Because the maturity of these contracts is staggered, a downturn in demand would have an impact on the lease agreements signed during that downturn. Of course, rates could rise during an economic boom.

Occupancy rates

A severe economic meltdown could not only result in reduced rates but a lower occupancy level. Because many REITs are diversified geographically, weak economic conditions in one area could be offset somewhat by better economic conditions in other areas.

Diversification

Some REITs specialize in specific types of real estate including office buildings, commercial buildings, industrial buildings, hotels, retirement homes and apartment complexes. As with equities, diversification among different real estate markets, both by the type of real estate and geographically, will reduce volatility and risk.

At any point in time one geographic area of the country may experience strong economic growth while another area is weak. Having broad geographic exposure helps to ensure that you don't have all of your eggs in the wrong basket. The same applies to the type of real estate. There are times when the demand for office space is weak but the demand for industrial space is strong and vice versa.

Prudent financial management would ensure that your investments are diversified rather than concentrated.

PRECIOUS METALS

THE PRECIOUS METALS market is generally considered to be gold, silver and platinum. Silver and platinum also have widespread industrial use, leaving gold as the purest definition of a precious metal.

The yellow metal is loved by some and hated by others. The middle ground has been hard to find. It has been around since the beginning of time and simply refuses to disappear, despite the best efforts of some governments and central banks to make it obsolete.

Gold is misunderstood. Its detractors see it as a lump of metal that doesn't have many uses and will sit in a safety deposit box, paying no dividends or interest. What can possibly make it attractive?

For one thing, gold should be treated as a currency rather than an investment. Like gold, a dollar doesn't pay any interest unless it is loaned out. Our financial system has made it easy to loan dollars; the borrowers pay **rent** on the dollars in the form of interest. Gold loans are less common.

A more fair comparison would be if an investor put a $100 bill in his safety deposit box along with a gold coin, both would earn the same rate of interest - zero.

Gold has one feature that makes it appealing over paper currency; it cannot be diluted or produced out of thin air.

Theoretically, the amount of money created by a country in a given year should be equivalent to the amount of goods and services it has produced. Yet by the end of 2012 many governments and their central banks had been printing money at an unprecedented rate without the corresponding level of economic activity. Without getting technical, the currency of these countries is diluted when unwarranted printing of money occurs.

Some refer to such activities as legalized counterfeiting. It is easy to "turn on the printing presses" and create more money without any justification for doing so. On the other hand, it is impossible to exponentially increase the amount of gold in the world. As a currency, it has held its purchasing power over the long term much better than paper dollars.

Gold, like every other asset class, has periods of time when it is in favour and periods of time when it is out of favour. Those who dismiss gold in an offhand manner may not have taken the time to understand its role in the world's monetary system.

Those who like gold regardless of the circumstances are often labeled 'gold bugs'. Unfortunately, those who recognize that gold comes into favour from time to time and then falls out of favour as circumstances change are also labelled gold bugs or speculators when they recommend gold.

There are points in time when it makes sense to own gold in a portfolio and other times when it does not make sense. Those who fail to recognize that and dismiss gold as a 'barbaric relic' may not have taken the time to understand the role it plays. If it hasn't disappeared as a financial asset in the past 10,000 years it is unlikely it will disappear in the near future.

The reason that gold is an important asset class is that it adds an element to a portfolio that no other investment provides.

Few investors or governments want gold to succeed because it often means everything else is a mess. But it also means that gold acts unlike anything else in a portfolio, making it the ideal complement to the other asset classes. However, there still seems to be no moderate position with regard to this asset.

Gold bugs can point to those cataclysmic periods in time where gold was the only investment that held its value. There have been periods of currency devaluation in Argentina, Germany and even the United States where gold was one of the few asset classes that held its value as the currencies became almost worthless. With hyperinflation rampant, **one ounce of gold** reached a value equal to **several trillion German marks** in 1923.

Detractors will similarly select periods where gold has performed poorly to make their case. In January 1980 the price of gold peaked around $850 per ounce before declining to just over $250 in September of 1999.

The truth lies somewhere between these two extremes. There will be times when an investment in gold will deliver great returns and times when it will fall in value. Of course, that is true with almost all investments. Trying to determine when that might happen is always difficult but gold presents special challenges.

Gold's Unique Role

Gold doesn't do anything. It has no earnings and no debt; it generates no profits and no losses. Gold has no employees, few industrial uses and doesn't rust. It is just a relatively rare and indestructible lump of metal.

But all of those shortcomings also make it very attractive. Its rarity means that a sudden supply won't be dumped onto the market to disrupt the supply/demand ratio. Its limited industrial use ensures a large amount of gold will not disappear into the manufacturing process and once again upset the supply/demand ratio. Its indestructibility means no special care must be taken to ensure its long term viability. Gold cannot be created from thin air, counterfeited or diluted. It remains constant.

Another feature of gold that makes it attractive as a currency is the fact that it is easily divisible without losing any value. In the barter system, it is difficult to trade a half a cow. Using other 'rare' commodities such as diamonds also has its drawbacks. Value is lost if a large diamond is split into smaller diamonds.

If all of these characteristics make gold sound like a foolproof currency, then you would be right. It can't be tampered with and therefore would impart a discipline on governments to manage their economies in an efficient manner. There would be no cheating by printing extra dollars, Euros or pounds to make up for shortfalls or bad decisions.

Problems would be dealt with before they spiraled out of control and sacrifices would be endured in the present rather than passed on to future generations and future governments.

Even if governments refuse to use gold or gold-backed 'dollars' as their currency, precious metals still have a role. Currencies are often measured relative to one another. The Canadian dollar, for example, is often quoted in terms of the US dollar. But what if both countries are devaluing their currency in an effort to solve economic problems? It may look like both are maintaining their value but the reality is that both are falling in value. In other words, both currencies are losing purchasing power, although it may not be apparent.

Like the general public, some financial advisors embrace gold and others avoid it. Investors who believe that there is some merit to investing a portion of their portfolio in gold at the appropriate time should be aware of the pros and cons of investing in the precious metal.

Investing in gold bullion can be accomplished through the purchase of physical coins or bars, through exchange traded funds or through mutual funds. The best choice will depend on the investor and their unique circumstances.

Valuation of gold

Gold may be the most difficult of all asset classes to value and that is one of the reasons why so many portfolio managers, advisors and investors stay away from it. They simply can't get a handle on it.

Part of the problem is that gold seems to be most frequently measured against cash, bonds or equities. A more accurate comparison may be to measure it against dollars, Euros or yen. These are all currencies, as is gold. Dollars don't earn dividends or interest; it is only when those dollars are lent out or used to purchase shares in a company that they earn a rate of return. The same applies to gold and that is how it should be compared.

Here is an experiment. Take a $100 bill and a piece of gold, put them both in a safety deposit box and open it a year later. If dollars really grew on their own, there might be a $5 bill or a $10 bill sitting next to the $100 bill. Currencies don't earn a rate of return and gold as a currency doesn't earn a rate of return either.

Some argue that the bank pays interest on dollars, contradicting the above argument. But a dollar deposited into a bank account is actually a loan to the bank. They turn around and lend that dollar to someone who wants to borrow it and earn a profit by charging a higher rate than they are paying.

It gets better. There is a practice that is approved by governments and central banks. It is known as fractional reserve lending. When you deposit your dollar into a bank, they loan it out not once but several times. If a significant portion of the population suddenly decided to withdraw their money from the bank they would find it wouldn't be there. Our Canadian banks would not be immune.

The entire fractional reserve system is built on promises and trust. The example above is simply used to illustrate that dollars, left on their own, do not earn interest. They are simply a tool that makes the exchange of goods and services more efficient.

Gold is another tool that serves that same purpose.

In order to accurately and objectively measure the value of a currency, it needs to be compared to a standard that does not change rather than another currency which is also changing. Once again, the characteristics of gold make it the ideal measuring stick.

There is always the temptation to discredit the measuring stick when the measurement is not as good as expected. Conspiracy theorists will say that this is exactly what is happening in the gold market. High gold prices are an indictment of central bank monetary policy and the theory exists that some governments are trying to suppress the price of gold to save the reputation of their currency.

An obscure but simple ratio between two financial statistics is one indicator that might be helpful in determining whether or not gold is an investment worth considering. It is the ratio between short term interest rates and the inflation rate. If interest rates are lower than the rate of inflation, the environment is positive for gold; if the situation is reversed, gold is less attractive.

The logic is also simple. If interest rates are lower than inflation, the currency loses purchasing power over time, despite the fact that interest is being earned on the investment. Investors begin to look for options and gold is one of those.

Other factors can come into play as well, but being aware of the ratio between interest rates and inflation is a good place to start.

Gold is not shares in gold mining companies

It is also important to keep in mind that there is a difference between physical gold and shares in gold mining companies. One is a precious metal, while the other is an equity, and the two can react very differently to the same economic events.

MUTUAL FUNDS, SEGREGATED FUNDS & EXCHANGE TRADED FUNDS

Investors can also participate in the various asset classes by purchasing a basket of individual investments through a mutual fund or exchange traded fund (ETF).

Some of these are passive investments, meaning they always hold the same stocks regardless of market conditions. Others are active investments, meaning the manager of the fund is constantly looking to take advantage of opportunities and avoid risk by analyzing the prospects of many different companies.

Mutual Funds

While a great deal of emphasis has been put on index funds and exchange traded funds as a low cost way to achieve diversification, these are typically passive investments. In other words, the individual investments within the funds seldom change. Actively managed mutual funds, on the other hand, use a combination of fundamental and technical analysis to choose the individual investments for their portfolios.

Active management can add value in market sectors or geographical areas where conditions can change rapidly and portfolios need to be adjusted.

Investing in intermediate sized oil companies, mining companies and technology companies offers great opportunity; however, these sectors require extreme diligence and it is best to have a portfolio manager to monitor their progress.

The same applies to the emerging markets where governments, economies and markets change more quickly than in developed markets. These are high growth areas but they are also areas that shouldn't be bought and then ignored. It pays to keep a watchful eye for both risks and opportunities.

Similarly, the high yield bond market requires diligence when it comes to monitoring the financial position of the companies issuing the bonds. And in the bond market, managers must always be on the watch for new opportunities as bonds within their portfolios mature.

Active management can be a benefit in all of these situations.

As with any asset class, investors should use the combination of active management, passive management and individual investments that best suit their particular situation.

Valuation

Over the past few years the result has been a growing level of discontent as many mutual funds have seen large redemptions. The problem hasn't been with the mutual funds themselves but with the equity markets. A large percentage of investors choose equity based mutual funds and when the equity markets provide returns near zero over a ten year period, even the best managers won't be able to generate great returns.

But investors "have heard" that mutual funds are bad investments and "have also heard" that dividend paying stocks are good, so there has been an exodus from funds into individual stocks. While these investors have experienced some success, it has little to do with mutual funds being bad investments and individual stocks being good investments.

Mutual funds are not inherently bad investments; it is simply that many were chosen based on their past performance rather than with an eye to the future. As a result, too much emphasis may have been placed on mutual funds in one asset class and too little emphasis placed on investments in others.

Over the past ten years, for example, mutual funds that invested in corporate bonds, real estate investment trusts, and gold bullion have performed extremely well. Equity funds, on the other hand, were deeply disappointing in most cases.

Investors will often still buy mutual funds **based on past performance** even when the economic conditions of the past look nothing like the current conditions nor are they likely to resemble the economic conditions of the future. Historical performance of mutual funds should only be used to *compare their results* with those of their peers and not used to project any future performance.

Mutual funds cannot be lumped into one category and evaluated on that basis. Ensure that you are making your judgments on an objective basis. A properly diversified portfolio of mutual funds, taking into consideration the factors previously discussed, can be used to build an excellent portfolio.

In the past, one of the primary uses for mutual funds was to invest in the broad equity markets. With the advent of technology and the introduction of new products such as ETFs, that role has been somewhat diminished but mutual funds are still a very important investment that can contribute to a portfolio. For some, they still represent the most viable investment option.

Despite higher management expense ratios (MERs) than exchange traded funds, mutual funds often represent the best alternative for smaller investors trying to build a balanced portfolio because purchases can be made in small amounts without incurring disproportionately high commissions.

SEGREGATED FUNDS

The life insurance industry participates in the investment business through their offerings of segregated funds or 'seg funds'. These investments are similar to mutual funds in that both represent a pool of funds that investors pay into and an independent manager makes the decisions regarding the investments held within the pool. However, seg funds, unlike mutual funds, are overseen by the insurance industry.

One difference between segregated funds and mutual funds is that seg funds offer a small degree of protection against investment loss. Most seg funds will guarantee 75% to 100% of the premiums paid, but there is a catch. Typically, the investment has to be held for a period of ten years before the guarantee comes into effect. Alternatively, the benefit would also apply on the death of the policy holder.

While this guarantee might provide some level of comfort, you would be hard pressed to find a blue chip equity or balanced mutual fund that was worth less than 75% of its value after holding it for ten years. In some ways, the guarantee is a red herring. For the privilege of guaranteeing a loss of no more than 25% of your portfolio over a minimum holding period of ten years, you would pay an annual management fee that is significantly higher than an equivalent mutual fund.

Those who use seg funds as an investment from which to derive income may lose significant guarantee benefits. In this case you may think you are buying a guarantee but the truth is that the guarantee may be much different from what you think it is. Red flags should go up if your financial advisor glosses over this fact.

The primary benefit to investing in seg funds is related to estate planning issues because you can name a beneficiary for your seg fund investment. Beneficiaries will usually receive the greater of the guarantee death benefit or the market value of the fund-holder's share without going through probate.

Before making an investment in a seg fund, ensure that you are aware of all the features, benefits and disadvantages of this choice compared to other investments available.

Exchange Traded Funds

Exchange traded funds or ETFS are similar to mutual funds in that they are a basket of individual investments put together to provide investors with an easy way to diversify. A major difference is that ETFs are bought and sold on stock exchanges such as the TSX, while a mutual fund is purchased from or sold to the mutual fund company that manages that fund.

When you buy or sell units in a mutual fund you don't know what the price will be. The fund is valued at the end of each day and that is the price you will pay for a purchase or receive for a sale. ETFs are traded continuously through the course of a trading day and you can set a price at which you are willing to buy or sell. They trade in a similar to manner to individual stocks.

Mutual funds will tend to have a higher management expense ratio (MER) than ETFs.

Exchange traded funds tend to have a lower management expense ratio (MER) than mutual funds; however, in a commission based account, there will be a fee charged when you buy an ETF and another fee charged when you sell it. When comparing mutual funds and ETFs, you have to consider any trading commissions in addition to the MER of each investment.

CHOOSING YOUR ASSET ALLOCATION

THE TEMPTATION EXISTS for investors to immediately start choosing individual stocks, bonds, mutual funds or ETFs (exchange traded funds) for their portfolios. In fact, this is where many investors start. They may have heard of a promising stock or scoured the financial pages for a top performing mutual fund. Unfortunately, they are investing without a plan and without taking into account the principles of building a suitable portfolio.

Actually, this approach is closer to speculating than investing, even if the investment chosen is not particularly aggressive.

The next step should be to determine the proper balance of investments in your account; in other words, it should be to determine the appropriate allocation among the various asset classes.

THE PROPER BALANCE

The analogy of a balanced diet can be revisited. Everyone needs protein, carbs, fats, vitamins and minerals; it is just that at different stages of our life, the balance among them should differ. The same applies to building a portfolio. The investment assets need to be allocated properly to suit the needs of the individual client. How much, if any, should be allocated to equities, to fixed income or to gold?

If you have completed a risk tolerance (investment profile) questionnaire, you will already know whether you are more conservative, equally conservative, or more aggressive than the average investor. Even with that information in hand, translating it into a suitable asset allocation is the next challenge.

One may think an investment in shares of a Canadian bank is a conservative investment, while others think a five year GIC is aggressive. Both would be wrong. Guidelines are needed to allow you to build the portfolio that matches your needs.

Most questionnaires not only provide the investor with a profile, they will suggest an asset allocation that fits with the profile. Even if the questionnaire does not generate any suggestions for asset allocation, you can seek the advice of a financial advisor to interpret that information and provide you with recommendations.

Asset Allocation - Rule of Thumb

Previously, I mentioned that a rule of thumb which is often used to determine a basic asset allocation is the age factor. It is worth reviewing.

Using this rule of thumb, the investor's age would equal the percentage of the portfolio allocated to bonds. A 40 year old would have a portfolio that has an allocation of 40% in bonds, while a 60 year old would have an allocation of 60% in bonds.

Using this rule of thumb, the investor would then allocate the remainder of the portfolio to equities.

Investors who felt they were more conservative than average would have an allocation to bonds that was higher than their age. Conversely, a more aggressive investor would have an allocation to bonds that was lower than their age. Using this approach, investors must determine whether they are more conservative, more aggressive or about average.

It is a simplistic method to determine asset allocation and certainly better than randomly selecting investments regardless of asset class. For investors who have never paid attention to asset allocation, it can be a quick way to check their portfolio.

Although it is better than nothing, one shortcoming with that rule of thumb is that it doesn't provide any guidance on how much should be allocated to the other asset classes. It only suggests a mix between fixed income and equities. The questionnaire that you use should provide more specific guidelines.

Sometimes, less is more. The categorization of six asset classes allows for a more clearly defined big picture than trying to incorporate fifteen or more asset classes. At a glance, you can determine if your mix of assets is reasonable. From there you can examine the investments within each asset class, knowing that the big picture is where it should be.

Once you are comfortable with your asset allocation decision, volatility can be further squeezed out of a portfolio by prudent investment decisions within each asset class. Careful selection of the specific investments can also improve your chances of increasing the return on your overall portfolio.

Risk Adjusted Returns

Investopedia (www.investopedia.com) defines risk adjusted returns as *"a concept that refines an investment's return by measuring how much risk is involved in producing that return"*. Generally speaking, risk is considered to be the amount of volatility associated with a given investment and various statistical measures can be used to measure that volatility.

It is important to remember that adding value doesn't mean achieving better returns; it means achieving better risk-adjusted returns. If two investments have identical long term rates of return but the first is highly volatile while the second is relatively stable, then the second investment has better risk-adjusted returns. You can count on the second investment to meet your expectations much more consistently than you can count on the first.

When comparing the performance numbers of any investments, consider the volatility along with the performance. The following chart illustrates the risk and return characteristics of a variety of investments. A higher position on the chart indicates a better return; the farther right the position, the greater the risk (volatility) of the investment. The trend line indicates a reasonable return for the amount of risk within the investment. Those investments that fall above the line have a superior risk/return profile than those that fall below the line.

The risk return profile for most investments can be plotted on a chart to help you visualize those investments that have done well and those whose performance has not justified the amount of risk to which you have been exposed.

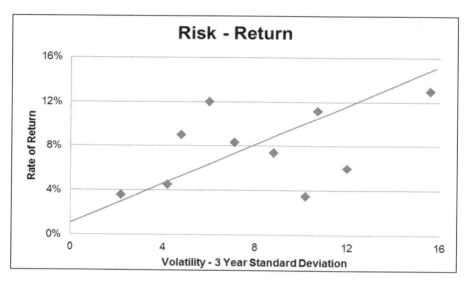

Rebalancing

Even investors who take a passive approach to their asset allocation will see that allocation drifts away from your starting point (the baseline) over time. Asset classes all grow at different rates and, left untouched, a portfolio will become skewed toward the best performing asset class and away from the poorest performing asset class.

Approximately once a year, or when new cash is added to a portfolio, the asset allocation should be reviewed to ensure that it is still close to the baseline. Another instance of when rebalancing should occur is when there has been a significant move in one or more of the asset classes.

Choosing your asset allocation

There should always be some leeway from your ideal asset mix or you would be constantly rebalancing and have time in your life for little else.

A side effect of rebalancing is that it forces the investor to sell a portion of their investments at a high price (the best performers) and replace them with low priced assets (those that have had the poorest performance). It is a strategy of selling high and buying low. This investment discipline helps to moderate volatility and can improve returns over time.

Examples

The best approach is to complete a risk tolerance questionnaire that suggests an appropriate asset mix. Failing that, some general guidelines using only three asset classes and three investment profiles can help to point you in the right direction.

Profile	Cash*	Fixed Income*	Equities*
Conservative	10% to 20%	45% to 65%	30% to 50%
Moderate	5% to 15%	25% to 45%%	45% to 65%
Aggressive	0% to 10%	5% to 25%	70% to 90%

Keep in mind that these asset mixes don't make any allowance for age or many other factors. They simply serve as a starting point from which you, or your advisor, can begin to formulate an appropriate asset mix.

Notes:

- An inverted yield curve is the situation that occurs when short term interest rates are higher than long term rates. An economic recession often follows when the situation of an inverted yield curve occurs.
- Long term bonds fluctuate in value more than short term bonds.
- While it seems counter intuitive, bond prices fall when interest rates rise and bond prices rise when interest rates fall.
- The total return on a bond is comprised of the interest plus or minus the change in price, if any.
- Preferred shares are more closely related to bonds than to common shares.
- The benchmark for the Canadian stock market (S&P/TSX Composite Index) does not include preferred shares or real estate investment trusts.
- The average value of the stock market over the past 110 years has been about 16x the average annual earnings. The ratio is known as the PE ratio.
- The PE ratio has been below 10x and above 40x on several occasions.
- Investor psychology/expectations result in valuations that are far different from the long term averages.
- Equities have tended to go through long periods of above average growth, known as secular bull markets, followed by long periods of below average growth, known as secular bear markets.
- These secular trends can last for 10 to 15 years or more.

- REITs allow for participation in a wide variety of real estate holdings.
- The value of REITs can be affected by mortgage rates, rental or lease rates and occupancy rates.
- Gold has several features that make it attractive as a currency.
- When interest rates are below the level of inflation, gold becomes an attractive alternative to paper currencies.
- Hyperinflation describes periods of extreme inflation where the purchasing power of a currency erodes quickly and can be a result of a government printing more money than is justified by the growth in its economy.
- Many categories of mutual funds achieved excellent returns during the economic downturn from 2008 to 2012.
- Calculating risk adjusted returns involves taking the volatility of the investment into consideration.
- Segregated funds can be useful as an estate planning tool.
- Choosing the appropriate asset allocation is the key first step to investment success; choosing specific investments within those asset classes is the second step.
- The historical risk/return profile of individual investments can be measured and plotted on a chart to provide a visual reference.
- Rebalancing is the process that returns the investments within your portfolio back to the desired asset allocation when it begins to deviate from your original strategy.

QUESTIONABLE INVESTMENTS & STRATEGIES

Invariably, investors hear about a better mousetrap – an investment or strategy that promises higher returns, lower taxes or a quicker route to financial independence. These ideas often subject the investor to additional risk in one form or another and should be examined with a skeptical eye.

A risk-free investment

A good place to start the conversation about questionable investments is to discuss a risk-free investment. It provides a great contrast to many risky strategies that may seem appealing on the surface.

Canadians who earn $50,000 per year will pay 30% to 35% tax on each dollar of **interest they earn** but they pay **no tax** on each dollar of **interest they save.**

Take the example of a homeowner who has a 5% mortgage. It would take an interest rate of about 7.5% to generate an after-tax return of 5% in a taxable account and in 2012 there were no guaranteed investments that paid anywhere close to 7.5%. On the other hand, if that money was used to pay down the mortgage, the homeowner has saved 5% after tax because he is no longer paying interest on that money. It is a risk-free way to save 5% after tax.

While there is *a chance* the homeowner could make in excess of 7.5% by investing his money rather than paying down the mortgage, it is not a risk-free investment. With all returns on investment, investors should consider the amount of risk that must be assumed in pursuit of that return.

The strategy of paying down your mortgage is the *opposite* of those who advocate taking out a home equity line of credit and investing the money in the pursuit of high returns. Investing with borrowed money is a *high risk / low return strategy,* while paying down your mortgage is a *low risk / high return strategy.*

Once the mortgage is paid, you can begin to invest additional funds in a portfolio tailored to meet your needs and not the needs of a banker or a mutual fund salesperson.

Your home as an investment for retirement

Because real estate is typically a very large investment financed with borrowed money (leveraged), it is worth spending considerable time on this topic.

Recently, many people, aided and abetted by the real estate industry and facilitated by the banking industry, have tended to adopt the idea that *my home is my retirement plan.* In doing so, they have purchased homes that are in excess of their needs because in their minds, a bigger home will lead to a bigger retirement.

High real estate prices have created a false sense of wealth. The United States has already gone through the painful process of a correction in real estate values. Many of those who expected to sell their homes for a handsome profit and retire on the proceeds have had their dreams shattered. As US real estate prices dropped, many homeowners were left with mortgages greater than the value of their homes.

We should learn from their experience.

While the price of housing in the US is now at much more reasonable levels, prices in Canada remain stubbornly high. Not only are real estate prices high in Canada, many Canadians are carrying disproportionately high mortgages and have been borrowing against the equity in their homes. Should real estate prices falter, that equity could be wiped out and banks could demand additional payments.

In June 2011 Mark Carney, the Governor of the Bank of Canada, made the following observation in a speech to the Vancouver Board of Trade. The full text of his commentary is available at http://www.bankofcanada.ca/wp-content/uploads/2011/06/sp150611.pdf.

Some of the key points made included:

*The ratio between the all-in monthly costs of owning a home and renting a home, as measured in the CPI, is close to its **highest level** since these series were first kept in 1949.*

*Financial vulnerabilities have increased as a result. Canadians are now as indebted (relative to their income) as the Americans and the British. The Bank estimates that the proportion of Canadian households that would be **highly vulnerable to an adverse economic shock** has risen to its highest level in nine years, despite improving economic conditions and the ongoing low level of interest rates.*

*This partly reflects the fact that the **increase in aggregate household debt** over the past decade has been driven by households with the highest debt levels.*

Instead of directing some of their excess income into savings, many Canadians have sunk all their savings into a larger home with the idea that they will sell the house upon retirement for a huge profit and live happily ever after on the proceeds.

In the minds of many investors, the arguments for this practice are tempting:

- Instead of throwing away money on rent, I am building equity.
- Real estate always goes up.
- There is no capital gains tax on the sale of a principal residence.

There are other facts and historical evidence that need to be examined:

- A bigger house than necessary comes with bigger expenses than necessary, including taxes, maintenance, utilities.

- Using your home as a retirement plan at the expense of other investments violates the principle of diversification.

- A mortgage is a highly leveraged investment. The risk of leverage will also be discussed later as a questionable investment strategy.

- Massive corrections in the price of housing in Japan, Spain and the United States illustrate the danger in this strategy.

This is not to say that real estate is a bad investment or that home ownership is wrong, but mixing these two separate ideas into one strategy is a dangerous practice. As many home owners in the US have learned, life savings can be completely wiped out in this very seductive scheme.

Anecdotal stories abound about those who failed to get into the real estate market and are now doomed to rent a second grade apartment for the rest of their lives. While that may happen in some cases, it is far from the norm.

Over the very long term, the value of a home cannot rise much more than the rate of inflation or the growth in wages. If it did, the cost of home ownership would eventually represent such a high percentage of income that there would be little left for other expenses. While there will be times when the housing market is under-valued, there will also be times that it is over-valued and generally speaking the long term rise in house values is very modest.

Growth in the value of real estate

Robert Shiller is a professor of economics at Yale and he confirms that claim. The following chart is derived from his website www.irrationalexuberance.com and it illustrates the change in the value of house prices over and above inflation.

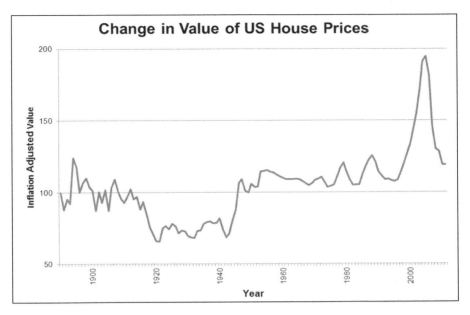

Source: www.irrationalexuberance.com

The results may surprise you:

- The average annual growth from 1890 to 2011 was about 0.20% per year above inflation.

- The average annual growth from 1890 to the peak in house values in 2005 was about 0.60% per year above inflation

- The average annual growth from the lowest values in 1920 to the peak in 2005 was about 1.30% per year above inflation

Simple logic indicates that growth in the value of real estate that is significantly above the growth rate in the economy (growth in GDP) is not sustainable in the long term. If that were to happen, housing would eventually become unaffordable and prices would fall back to the point where it ***does*** become affordable. Mark Carney's comments seem to bear this out.

From 2001 to 2010 house prices in Canada rose at a pace of approximately

7.5% per year. During the same period, GDP rose by only 2.9% per year. House prices became increasingly unaffordable during this period. Two solutions to the problem of unaffordable housing are rapidly increasing incomes (unlikely in this economic environment) or falling house prices.

In his comments to the Vancouver Board of Trade, Mark Carney, Governor of the Bank of Canada, also commented that over the long term house prices in Canada have averaged about **3.5x median income**. As of June 2011 they were about **4.5x median income**. While the ratio varies from city to city and there will always be exceptions or pockets of opportunity, the overall picture for the potential growth in residential real estate values is dim.

If prices were to return to 3.5x median income, it would require a correction of about 23%.

Expecting growth in the value of an investment that may already be overvalued is optimistic at best and dangerous at worst. If real estate is truly over-valued by 23%, counting on the long term growth in the value of your home to fund retirement could lead to disappointment. The lesson in this is that your primary residence should be viewed as a place to live, rather than as an investment.

As a simple test, subtract about 23% from the current value of your home and see how you feel about your financial situation. Would you still have equity in your home or do you now owe more than the value of the mortgage? Were you planning on withdrawing equity from your home in the form of a line of credit? Would you still have the ability to do that? A lot of plans can be derailed by those counting on real estate values to fund their lifestyle and their retirement.

As mentioned earlier, evidence of what can happen when real estate becomes unaffordable can be seen by looking at what has happened in the United States since 2007.

In Canada our aging demographic is another factor that could affect the resale value of homes in the future. The Baby Boomers represent a disproportionately large percentage of the population and this group will ultimately downsize or move retirement homes. The pool of buyers available to buy these homes is smaller than the pool of potential sellers.

Rental properties

Rental properties are another story. Owning them is a business asset that should be evaluated on the basis of their ability to create positive cash flow and is beyond the scope of this discussion. One point to keep in mind is that owning rental properties is an active business that requires a great deal of time, while investing is a more passive strategy that requires far less time and physical effort.

Comparing ownership of rental properties to a portfolio of investments is like comparing apples and oranges. Despite their differences, both can help you reach your financial goals if managed properly.

Reverse Mortgages

While on the topic of real estate, it is worthwhile to discuss reverse mortgages.

Retirees who have built significant equity in their homes over time can be tempted to tap into that equity to supplement their retirement income. Rather than making a mortgage payment and reducing their liability, those who implement a reverse mortgage are, in effect, withdrawing a mortgage payment and increasing their liability.

The interest charged on this mortgage withdrawal can be very high and in some cases it is compounded annually. Over time the equity in your home can be devoured by withdrawals and accumulated interest. If your personal situation unexpectedly changes, that could be a devastating development.

An article that appeared in Money Sense magazine outlines some of the risks involved in taking out a reverse mortgage. You can read it at http://www.moneysense.ca/2007/12/03/the-mortgage-that-grows/. According to the article, once you have adopted the strategy, "you can't change your mind".

Given the possibility that house prices in Canada may be over-valued as of 2012, additional caution should be exercised.

Before you are dazzled by the potential benefits of a reverse mortgage, learn more about any potential pitfalls and what alternatives may be more appropriate.

Leverage

Encouraging investors to take out a loan in order to invest in mutual funds is a strategy that has been advocated by some advisors. The rationale is that the loan interest is tax deductible and that the returns on the mutual fund will be higher than the interest rate on the loan. It is presented as a win-win situation.

With interest rates at historically low levels, this strategy can become even more tempting.

The first risk is that returns in the stock market may be less than you expect. In the ten year period from 2000 to 2010 the equity markets in Canada, the United States and Europe provided almost no return to the investor. That would have been ten years of paying interest with nothing to show for it.

Proponents of this strategy say that the markets will always rebound and go up in the long term. It is a self-serving statement. Markets can go sideways for a long time and some have even shown long term declines in value. For example, the Japanese stock market includes such iconic names as Honda, Toyota, Panasonic and Sony; yet it has been in a state of decline for twenty years. While that may not happen in Canada, the fact remains that it could.

The second risk is interest rates. While rates may be low now, the situation can change quickly and severely. Interest rates are directly tied to inflation which is directly tied to the amount of money a government prints... and in the period between 2007 and 2012 a lot of money has been printed. In other words, interest rates could rise at the worst possible time for someone implementing a leveraged investment strategy.

While the stock market often benefits from inflation, it doesn't help the investor if those gains are offset by skyrocketing interest rates.

The third risk is timing. It may be that you need to cash in your investments to cover an emergency expense or perhaps a job loss or illness makes it impossible to service your loan payments. Equity markets are volatile and if an unfortunate circumstance occurs when the markets are in the midst of a correction, it can prove extremely costly.

Three out of four people are likely to make money on a mutual fund leverage strategy. The first is the banker who lends you the money, the second is the financial advisor who collects commissions he would not otherwise have earned and the third is the mutual fund company which collects the annual management fees on the funds you are holding. As the fourth person involved in this scheme, you can also make money with a leveraged investment, but you are taking all of the risk and you are at the bottom of the food chain.

It is never fun when you lose money on an investment; it is even worse when you lose money that you have borrowed and are saddled with payments with nothing to show for it. Be wary of anyone who promotes an investment strategy that includes investing in mutual funds or stocks using borrowed money.

Leveraged and Inverse ETFs

Some exchange traded funds (ETFs) use alternative investment strategies that can involve leverage (borrowing to invest). You may be unaware of these loans but they are embedded in the structure of the fund. These ETFs are subject to significantly greater volatility than non-leveraged ETFs and can result in substantial losses should market prices fall.

Inverse ETFs are designed to increase in value if market prices fall. Some inverse ETFs also use leverage, making them even more complex.

In many cases, the underlying investments are not stocks or bonds but rather they are future contracts. These types of products should only be used by highly sophisticated investors who have the ability to follow the markets closely and place trades very quickly. Even then, their value is questionable.

For the average investor, leveraged ETFs and inverse ETFs are products to avoid.

Labour Sponsored Venture Funds

Labour sponsored venture funds are a special class of mutual funds that have a tax credit associated with them. These funds invest in very small companies, many of them private companies that have limited access to capital to start or expand their business operations. As an incentive for investors to take the additional risk and invest in these companies, a tax credit for investing in these funds has been approved by the federal and provincial governments.

As with anything in the real world, there are no free lunches. Once the fund has been purchased and the tax credit claimed, the investor must hold on to the fund for **eight years** or be forced to repay the tax credit.

That is only part of the bad news. With a couple of exceptions, performance has generally been abysmal, the cost to manage these funds has been high and the expertise in the area of venture capital has been lacking.

An article published in the Globe and Mail on October 24, 2010 revealed that only 6 of 17 funds that had an eight year track record showed positive returns to the investor.

A paper released in March 2012 by the School of Public Policy at the University of Calgary called for an end to government funding of labour sponsored ventured funds. For those who want to take the time to read the findings of Professor Jeffrey MacIntosh, the link to the website is http://policyschool.ucalgary.ca.

Day Trading

This strategy involves buying and selling a stock on the same day. It has been facilitated by the low commission structures of discount brokers and online brokers. The unintended consequence was that large numbers of inexperienced investors were lured into the market where the prospect of quick profits and low fees promised easy riches.

And it worked...for a while. The late 90s were the days when the markets climbed exponentially higher day after day and stocks like Nortel were trading at over $200 per share. It really didn't matter much which stock you bought because they all went up. It created a false sense of security among investors and some even quit their jobs to focus on trading their own portfolios.

When the 'tech wreck' occurred early in the new millennium, many of the high flying stocks crashed to earth, destroying the wealth of numerous day traders. Unable to sell at a profit by the end of the day, some would hold on, hoping for a bounce in price. Instead, prices cascaded lower day after day and the glamorous image of day trading quickly became tarnished.

Yet advertisements still appear on television advocating trading strategies that will put you a step ahead.

Trading and investing are two completely different approaches that happen to participate in the same market. The average Canadian should probably be an investor – not a day trader. The cards are stacked against them when it comes to strategies like day trading.

The rise and fall of day trading may have served one purpose. It has clearly illustrated that low commissions do not guarantee success. In fact, it has shown that investors can be tempted into irrational behaviour when some of the barriers are removed.

RRSP Meltdown Strategy #1

This strategy is actually terrifying. It can work out unbelievably well, it can have minimal benefits or it can be financially crippling.

The idea is to collapse your RRSP account and withdraw all the money in the account. That immediately creates a huge tax bill but with the meltdown strategy, the investor takes the proceeds from the RRSP and purchases flow-through shares.

Without going into a lengthy explanation, flow-through shares are tax advantaged investments where the purchaser of the shares gets a big tax credit. The reason there is a tax credit associated with them is because the proceeds received from the sale of the shares is used in exploration projects in the energy and mining industries. These are considered high risk undertakings and to encourage investors to take risk, the government offers tax credits.

The theory is that the investor is able to get most of the money out of their RRSP while paying only minimal taxes. It may be very tempting but the key phrase is 'high risk'. If the exploration projects do not work out as well as hoped for, the value of flow through shares can plummet and in extreme cases become worthless.

Investors should not throw caution to the wind in an effort to avoid taxes and this strategy does exactly that. In an effort to save a few dollars in taxes some investors have invested inappropriate amounts of money in flow-through shares using this strategy.

It can work out and your advisor may point to past success, but make no mistake, an RSP meltdown strategy that uses flow-through shares to offset taxes is a high risk strategy.

RRSP Meltdown Strategy #2

This is another strategy of questionable merit. It involves taking out a bank loan and making an investment with the proceeds of that loan. Because the loan is for investment purposes the interest you pay is tax-deductible. The next step is to withdraw an amount from your RRSP each year that covers the interest cost on your loan. The tax on the RRSP withdrawal is offset by the tax-deductible interest.

The theory goes that your investments grow faster than the rate of interest on your loan over time and you have gradually withdrawn all the assets from your RRSP without paying any tax on those withdrawals. It can work if all the pieces fall into place but it is fraught with danger. For many who implemented the strategy at the beginning of the new millennium it has likely been an unmitigated disaster.

The problem with this strategy is that the investor is **once again using leverage** and betting their retirement on that leverage. It is a wolf in sheep's clothing.

Speculative Stocks

'Penny stocks' is a term synonymous with highly speculative low priced shares. They don't necessarily have to trade for pennies but many of these stocks have one thing in common... **they have no revenues,** never mind earnings (profits).

When you invest in companies that have no revenue, they are simply taking your money and working on a project in the hope that it will at some point become viable, generate some revenues and eventually realize a profit. Buying shares in companies at this stage of their development is the definition of speculation and has very little in common with buying shares of well-established companies that have a solid track record of earnings and growth.

Yet the temptation to abandon a disciplined strategy can increase when an investor hears a friend or colleague talking about a 'hot tip' and they begin to dream of remarkable returns.

Pursuing speculative investments is not a strategy that should be part of a long term financial plan. Investors who still want the rush of buying speculative stocks should set up a separate trading account for that purpose and should not cannibalize their retirement assets to fund the new account. These stocks are not appropriate investments if you are relying on them to fund your retirement.

Unfortunately, some investors will lump all stocks into the same category, shying away from a good company with solid earnings and a reasonable dividend because of a bad experience with a penny stock. While the ongoing viability of these companies compared to a 'penny stock' is as different as night is from day, they are painted with the same brush.

Hedge Funds

Investopedia (www.investopedia.com) defines hedge funds as funds that *"use advanced investment strategies such as leveraged, long, short and derivative positions in both domestic and international markets with the goal of generating high returns"*.

When it comes to investing, the term hedge should mean "hedging your risk" and that is what authentic hedge funds do; they hedge your risk. Unfortunately the strategies used to hedge risk can be mutated into a form that actually increases risk...exponentially!! Unfortunately this part the financial services industry is largely unregulated and a plethora of these highly volatile funds have been created. They should be tagged performance seeking hedge funds rather than risk management hedge funds.

Unfortunately, most hedge funds operate as a black box. In other words, the manager will rarely disclose exactly what they are holding and how these advanced strategies are being applied. For investors, that means they are buying something they cannot see and must rely on the managers' abilities to outsmart the market. While there are probably some very good hedge funds, there are also some very bad ones. Those that fail can fail in a spectacular manner, often because leverage is widely used in hedge funds and leverage can magnify losses as well as gains.

A good example is Long Term Capital Management, a hedge fund whose board of directors included former Nobel Prize winners in economics. Logic would seem to indicate that if anyone knew what they were doing it would be Long Term Capital Management. Stunningly, its failure in 1998 not only wiped out those who invested in the fund, it almost led to a collapse in the world financial markets.

The entire story can be read in the book by Roger Lowenstein, "When Genius Failed: The Rise and Fall of Long-Term Capital Management". Renowned financial writer and author of "Moneyball", Michael Lewis, also wrote about Long Term Capital Management in a 1999 New York Times article entitled "How the Eggheads Cracked".

Authentic hedge funds, on the other hand, can add stability to a portfolio but determining whether a fund is an authentic hedge fund or a performance seeking hedge fund is a difficult task. Your financial advisor can help.

One final note about hedge funds. Their fee structure usually differs substantially from the fee structure you may be used to with mutual funds. That is code for "the fees can be very high".

For the average investor, hedge funds are a questionable investment.

COMMODITIES

Physical commodities can be simply described as things that you can touch and feel; they have a physical presence. They include metals such as copper or nickel, foodstuffs such as grains, meats or orange juice and energy products such as crude oil or natural gas. The list of tradable commodities is extensive but few investors understand exactly how they trade.

When you trade commodities on a commodities exchange you are not buying the physical commodity. Rather, you are entering into a contract whereby you promise to buy and take delivery of that commodity at a future date at a pre-determined price. When you enter into that contract, you put up a 'good faith deposit', known as initial margin, which represents only a very small portion of the total value of the contract.

Once again, leverage is involved and in this case it is substantial.

Those who have a need for that commodity in the future (an end user) and who are willing to take delivery of the commodity would be classified as hedgers. An example may be a food processing company that wants to ensure it will be able to secure a supply of corn in the future at a predetermined price.

Those who have no need for the commodity in the future but who are simply expecting the price to rise are speculators. They hope the price will rise and they can sell their contract before the delivery date.

As an example, a speculator may have taken out one contract for crude oil with an initial margin payment of $9,000. If he has to take delivery of that contract, he must pay the full price for 1000 barrels of crude oil and must find a place to store those 1000 barrels (roughly 170,000 litres) until someone is willing to buy it from him. Depending on the price specified in the contract, the sums of money can be enormous. At $90 per barrel, the cost would be $90,000 plus storage.

Very few investors want to cough up an additional $90,000 on an initial investment of $9,000.

While this short explanation oversimplifies the commodities markets, it does serve to illustrate some of the challenges of investing in commodities. Be cautious and research the commodity markets extensively before considering an investment in this area.

Most of the familiar names among retail investment firms in Canada do not offer commodity trading services to their clients.

Company Shares

Investing in the shares of the company you work for can be a good idea; over-investing in those shares rarely is.

There have been too many cases where employees have the bulk of their life savings tied up in company shares. They are not only relying on the company to provide them with a paycheque, they are relying heavily on them for their retirement income as well. It is the extreme example of putting all of your eggs in one basket. Companies like Enron and Nortel are prime examples of what can go wrong with this strategy.

Part of the employee bias can be a result of loyalty to the company. It can also come from employees confusing their familiarity with the company with its potential, or it can come from unrealistic expectations regarding the industry in which the company operates.

In the case of loyalty, some employees strongly believe in the company they work for and conclude it would be disloyal not to own as many shares as possible if given the opportunity. They become emotionally tied to the company rather than looking at their situation in an objective manner.

Employees may also have a lot of confidence in their co-workers and their efforts to make the company a success. This familiarity with their own company often precludes a broad overview of the economy, the markets and other investment opportunities. Those who fall into this category tend to overlook the big picture.

The unrealistic expectations can stem from seeing the financial success that senior executives in their company achieved through share ownership. The circumstances under which their shares were acquired, however, may have been far different from those of a new employee. In addition, these shares may represent only a small portion of the total net worth of the executive.

There can also be an element of naïvety. Employees may understand the workings of their company but not how its value is perceived by the market. The relationship between a company's operations and its share price is not linear. The market can view and value a company far differently from an employee and it is the market price that counts.

While there is nothing wrong with owning company shares in a company that you work for and believe in, it needs to be kept in perspective. Perhaps **the biggest danger in this strategy** is that employees may have over half of their total investments held in the shares of their company. It is a situation known as portfolio concentration and it can subject the value of your portfolio to wild swings...both up and down.

The percentage of a portfolio held in shares of a single company should rarely exceed 10% of the total value of your investments and 5% is a far better guideline. If part of your compensation is in the form of company shares, monitor how much of your total portfolio these shares comprise. When the opportunity arises, adjust your holdings to appropriate levels and diversify your holdings using the principles discussed earlier.

Notes:

There is an old hockey adage that states, 'offense is exciting but defense wins championships'. The same theory applies to investing. When trying to achieve investment success, minimizing mistakes is as important as maximizing opportunities. It is about treating your money well.

The list of investment strategies that should be scrutinized closely or avoided altogether is relatively long. Some of these may be exciting and the rewards can be great, if you are lucky, but there is the potential to make a big mistake and jeopardize your financial health. These strategies include:

- Relying on an increase in the value of your home to fund retirement.
- Reverse mortgages.
- Leverage (borrowing to invest).
- Investing in leveraged and/or inverse ETFs.
- Investing in labour sponsored venture funds.
- Day trading.
- Investing in speculative (penny) stocks.
- RRSP meltdown strategies.
- Investing in hedge funds.
- Investing in commodities.
- Over-investing in the shares of the company you work for or the industry you work in.

SECTION FIVE

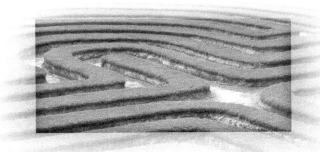

INSURANCE &
ESTATE PLANNING

INSURANCE

Insurance is one way to manage some of the risks we face in our lives. It won't prevent the tragic or unexpected from happening but it can help us deal with it. There are also other ways to manage some of these risks. The key is to understand what the risks are and the consequences of the options available for dealing with them, and then to be comfortable with your decision.

Insurance Overview

Insurance is a method of managing risk by sharing it with others and we pay a premium for the privilege of pooling that risk. In some cases, the purchase of insurance is mandated by regulations. We can't drive a car legally on public roads without having some form of insurance. Our basic health care costs are covered by premiums that are mainly paid for out of our taxes. Employment insurance premiums are taken from employers and employees before we ever see the money.

The benefits of insurance seem obvious. For a fee you can have a significant portion of expenses that you would otherwise be responsible for covered by a pool of money into which you and many others contribute. If that unexpected expense arises, then everyone helps pay for it through the premiums they have paid.

The disadvantages of insurance are less apparent. One drawback is the cost. Insurance companies are in the business of making money. They could not exist if their expenses exceeded their revenues and on top of all those expenses, the company must earn a profit for its investors. Although as an individual you may collect on a policy, it is impossible for everyone who buys insurance to ever recover their expenses (the premiums that have paid).

This is not to suggest that people should never buy insurance but to recognize that the voluntary purchase of insurance is not always the most cost effective approach. A closer examination of our lifestyles may reveal that insurance is appropriate in some instances but in other instances the risks can be more effectively managed through other means.

Keep in mind that should you decide upon insurance as a solution, the theory behind the purchase of insurance is that its purpose is to mitigate risk rather than to earn a return on investment.

Who Needs Life Insurance?

If you have dependents who are reliant on your income, they will continue to need financial support in the event that you die. In this case, a life insurance policy makes sense. Some examples are:

- If you are supporting a family, you need life insurance.
- If you have children, you need insurance at least until they finish college.
- If you have special-needs children, you might need a life insurance policy that will protect them at every age.
- If you have a non-working spouse, you need life insurance to protect your spouse at least until their government benefits, such as Old Age Security and other sources of retirement, kick in.

If you are single with no dependents, you **don't need life insurance** at all; certainly you don't need more than your employer might automatically provide. Don't let anyone tell you otherwise.

How Much Insurance Do You Really Need?

There is no one right answer to this question but a guideline might be 5 times your annual income plus enough to pay any outstanding mortgage and tuition fees for any post-secondary education your children may choose to pursue. If you have an employee-sponsored life insurance plan, it only needs to be supplemented to an appropriate level.

The death benefit that your beneficiaries receive is generally not subject to federal income tax or provincial income tax. The size of your policy should be based on your after-tax income because that is what you are used to living on.

Just as a banker makes more money by offering you the largest loan you can afford, the life insurance agent makes the most money by selling you the life insurance policy with the largest premiums. Know what you need and don't be oversold.

Term Insurance or Permanent Insurance

Cash-value policies are considered **permanent insurance** because the policies stay in effect as long as you continue to pay the premiums. **Term policies,** as the name implies, expire at a specified time.

Cancelling your policy

Make your choices carefully because cancelling an insurance policy is not like opting out of an investment plan. There is a good chance that you will get very little or none of your money back if you cancel that policy in its early years.

It may be shocking to find out how much of your money can disappear in sales commissions and related expenses if and when you go to cash in a permanent insurance policy. If you cancel your policy, you should do so cautiously, even if you no longer need life insurance. Administrative costs and agents' commissions can take so much of the cash value that what is left for you can be far less than you expect.

A study sponsored by the Life Insurance Marketing and Research Association (LIMRA) and the Society of Actuaries in 2005 found that nearly 40% of all individual life insurance policies lapse in the first five years.

Another study by LIMRA International in 2009 found that an average of about 7.5% of policy holders allowed their policies to lapse on an annual basis. Those who had their policies in place for a long period of time tended to allow policies to lapse at a lower rate while those with newer policies tended to allow their policies to lapse at a higher rate.

Other industry statistics indicate that almost 20% of all cash-value policies terminate in the first year, and that 40% terminate in the first 10 years or so because the policy owners fail to keep up premium payments. If you surrender some policies early on, you may get nothing and you may be required to pay surrender fees.

Common sense tells us that in the event of financial hardship policies with higher premiums are more likely to be cancelled than those with lower premiums. If you decide that life insurance is appropriate for your situation and decide to purchase a policy, try to ensure that you will be able to maintain your premium payments even when times are tough to prevent your policy from lapsing.

Term Insurance

If you check term insurance on Wikipedia, you will find the following definition:

> *Term life insurance . . . provides coverage at a fixed rate of payments for a limited period of time, the relevant term. After that period expires, coverage at the previous rate of premiums is no longer guaranteed and the client must either forgo coverage or potentially obtain further coverage with different payments or conditions. If the insured dies during the term, the death benefit will be paid to the beneficiary. Term insurance is the least expensive way to purchase a substantial death benefit on a coverage amount per premium dollar basis over a specific period of time.*

The key term is that it is the **least expensive way to purchase a substantial death benefit**. Since the entire purpose of life insurance is to provide a death benefit, term insurance makes a lot of sense...IF you need insurance.

Death benefits from a term insurance policy can be used to pay off your mortgage, fund the education of your children and provide income for your spouse. You don't need multiple policies to cover these liabilities; one policy will do and will likely be the least expensive approach. Banks, in particular, will often try to sell an expensive mortgage insurance policy to homebuyers.

Since term insurance is the least expensive insurance, the chances are that you will be out the least amount of money should you cancel your policy or should it lapse due to the non-payment of premiums.

Permanent Insurance

Permanent insurance (in contrast to term insurance) can have a tax-deferred "savings" feature of permanent insurance. These policies are often billed as investment and savings vehicles; however, they are not well-suited to achieving that end.

There are many variations of permanent insurance, each with a slightly different name, making the entire process a confusing one. Most of these policies are either whole life or universal life.

In simple terms, a ***whole life policy*** is a permanent policy in which the premiums are the same for the entire life of the policy. You accumulate a cash reserve within the policy but the insurance company, not you, decides where it is invested. Typically, the insurance company invests it in low-risk securities which generate a low return.

Universal life policies combine the protection of term insurance with a savings component and you will have some choice in how the savings component is invested.

Whatever kind of permanent life insurance policy you choose, the increase in value will often be modest at best. However, the life insurance industry has been able to commingle insurance policies with investments while keeping the structure less than transparent. It is confusing and those who buy a policy are often unaware of the details.

No matter how anyone tries to package it, life insurance is not an investment; it is life insurance and that is what it should be used for.

There can be one exception. A good cash-value (permanent insurance) policy can sometimes be used as a sophisticated *estate-planning tool*. Some of these strategies are appropriate if you're *a high-net-worth individual* and you are not worried about liquidity (access to your capital). An individual in this group would be in the highest marginal tax bracket even after making maximum RRSP contributions. That would include those who make in excess of $150,000 per year.

If you fit that category, life insurance can be an ideal wealth-transfer asset.

Be cautioned, however, because the federal government has been gradually changing the regulations and further changes could be made in the future. It is important to keep current with legislation surrounding life insurance before making a major long term commitment to a permanent insurance policy.

Permanent insurance policies are not great investment vehicles, other than the fact that they force you to save. The premiums are high and funding them reduces your available cash for other obligations. Some insurance agents promote buying permanent insurance policies on young children as a means to fund their future education. It is an expensive and inflexible approach. Unlike an investment program, if you cancel your permanent life insurance policy you may get very little or even none of your contributions back. It can be a 100% loss.

One common characteristic of these policies is that *you lose control of your capital.*

Insurance policies you don't need

Insurance for children

Life insurance purchased on children's lives is often an emotional choice rather than a logical choice. The definition of life insurance is that it provides income or a safety net for those dependent on the insured. Since you are not financially dependent upon your children, you should not carry insurance on their lives.

It is worth repeating that using permanent insurance as a means to fund their education is both inefficient and inflexible. A Registered Educational Savings Plan (RESP) is a better choice.

Mortgage life insurance

This type of insurance policy will pay off the mortgage on your house in the event of your death. As you pay down your mortgage, the amount of coverage is reduced by a similar amount. It is a declining benefit life insurance policy. For the same price, or even less in many cases, you can purchase a term policy where the death benefit remains constant even as your mortgage is paid down.

Mortgage life insurance is often encouraged by your bank or credit union because the high cost of premiums, along with the declining benefits, makes it very profitable for them.

RRSP insurance for retirees

There have been cases where investors have purchased a life insurance policy to "pay the tax" on their RRSP should they die. If the person holding the RRSP account has a spouse, then upon death the RRSP assets can be rolled over to that spouse tax-free. There is certainly no need for a life insurance policy in this case. If the person holding the RRSP account has no spouse, there will be no one reliant upon those assets for retirement income and no need for a life insurance policy.

Whether a life insurance policy is in place or not, **the government will collect any taxes** owed to them when an RRSP is collapsed. These taxes will be paid by the estate rather than the beneficiaries. Those who are insistent upon leaving an estate for their adult children may want to take out a life insurance policy but it should not be purchased under the misconception that it will somehow reduce the tax liability on the collapse of an RRSP.

This strategy does allow for *a larger estate* but you are buying insurance for reasons outside the definition of insurance. Premiums can be costly at this stage of life and money spent on these premiums is money that is unavailable for other lifestyle expenses.

Insurance policies you should have

Life insurance

It is important to reiterate that life insurance protects those people who are financially dependent on you. Examine your situation carefully and calculate what level of insurance will allow those who are dependent upon you to continue their lives with minimal interruption. Your life insurance agent can help you with those decisions.

Long term disability insurance

Many of us have long term disability insurance through a group plan at our place of employment. If you are not covered by a group plan, you should establish your own long term disability policy that would allow you to maintain a reasonable lifestyle if you were no longer able to continue working. If you are retired, you do not need long term disability insurance.

This type of insurance is not straightforward. Premiums can be burdensome and coverage can be limited, depending upon the policy you choose. It is critical that you work with an agent who is well versed in the nuances of long term disability insurance before choosing a policy.

Insurance policies you may want to consider

The insurance industry continues to broaden the range of products it offers. While life insurance provides financial payouts to the beneficiaries, there are two insurance policies that provide payouts to the policy holder. They are critical illness insurance and long term care insurance.

Critical Illness Insurance

Critical illness insurance typically provides for a payout to the policy holder if they are diagnosed with a critical illness covered by the policy. Pre-existing conditions may prevent you from buying a policy and some illnesses are not covered.

On the upside, the payout is tax-free and can be used for any purpose the policy holder sees fit. It does not have to be used for the treatment of a medical condition. Some policies provide for a refund of premiums after a pre-determined number of years or at a specific age. Of course, coverage also ends with the refund of premiums.

Before you purchase a critical illness policy, understand what is covered and what is not, understand any other features and limitations of the policy and be aware of what your premiums will be.

Because many critical illnesses that are covered by these policies tend to strike more frequently later in life, it is more appropriate to have coverage in the mid-adult period of life. Purchasing a critical illness policy early in life means it is highly likely that you will be paying years of premiums to cover an event that has a low probability of occurring.

Do your homework because there are significant differences from one policy to the next with respect to the level of premium payments, illnesses covered and other factors.

Long term care insurance

These policies help provide for long term care for those who may not be considered sick in the traditional sense of the word but who may require assistance in the daily activities of living.

These policies will provide financial assistance to individuals who require long term help with basic personal activities such as dressing, bathing, eating, getting in and out of bed or a chair, and even walking. The coverage can include adult day care, assisted living, nursing home care, home care and other levels of care. It cannot be purchased once the need for this kind of care is already established.

Long term care insurance can be one of the most complicated insurance policies to understand and the options for coverage and the premiums can vary widely from one insurer to the next.

As with life insurance policies, some people will let their critical illness and long term care policies lapse. They will pay the premiums while they are employed but may let the policies lapse when they feel they can't afford the premiums or when they retire. This would waste all of the money spent on premiums.

It is another reason to buy no more insurance than you can afford in the first place.

In 2012, some insurance companies quit offering long term care insurance. While the concept may be appealing, it may have been too generous. Check the availability and cost of long term care insurance before making any decisions.

Life Insurance if You Are Close to Retirement

If you are "empty nesters" with a house that's paid for and you both work or have other sources of income, it might make sense to spend your money on something besides life insurance.

However, you should consider life insurance close to retirement if you have any of the following:

- Young children.
- A disabled adult child.
- An outstanding mortgage on your home or vacation property.
- Any large outstanding loans, such as a home equity loan.
- A nonworking spouse who is much younger than you.

Once again, ensure that the level of insurance is appropriate and covers a suitable term.

Summary

There are numerous kinds of insurance designed to cover a multitude of misfortunes and there are countless variations among policies. While a certain amount of insurance coverage may be prudent or even necessary in many situations, they all cost money. In many cases, the premiums paid will never be recouped.

Before you buy any policy make sure you understand the coverage, the terms of the policy and the costs.

ESTATE PLANNING

Estate planning is an important topic that should be explored in more detail. A simple starting point is to complete a checklist, create a will and name an executor. While many Canadians have already created a will and given a great deal of thought to how they would like their estate handled, the role of the executor can be overlooked. And choosing the wrong executor can have its consequences.

For more details on estate matters, I encourage you to read "Estate Planning Through Family Meetings" by Lynne Butler.

Create a checklist

The first step in developing an estate plan/insurance strategy is to look at your current situation. This checklist can help you identify what you already have in place and what you might want to look at more closely. It can also assist your financial advisor or insurance agent in evaluating your situation and suggesting possible solutions.

Insurance and Estate Planning Checklist

		Yes	No	Unsure
1	Are your will and pre-estate documents up-to-date for health and financial matters?	☐	☐	☐
2	Are your executors and/or powers of attorney aware that you have named them for these roles?	☐	☐	☐
3	Have you named beneficiaries for your RRSPs, life insurance policies, LIFs and RRIFs, pension plans, and/or deferred profit sharing plans?	☐	☐	☐
4	Have you estimated your income tax due on death?	☐	☐	☐
5	Do you have dependents reliant upon your income?	☐	☐	☐
6	Do you have enough life insurance in place to pay your mortgage?	☐	☐	☐
7	Do you have life insurance and savings in place to cover at least 5x annual pre-tax income after your mortgage has been paid?	☐	☐	☐
8	Do you have long term disability coverage at your place of employment?	☐	☐	☐
9	Do you have enough insurance and savings to pay the cost of unexpected illness including home care, long term care or income taxes without forcing the sale of the family assets such as the house, cottage or family business?	☐	☐	☐
10	Have you prepared a living will or medical directive?	☐	☐	☐
11	Have you considered making a planned gift to charity?	☐	☐	☐
12	If you have a business, do you have a succession plan to ensure its future?	☐	☐	☐
13	Are there ways to simplify your financial affairs so your estate can be settled more quickly?	☐	☐	☐

While not all of these questions apply to every situation, they may generate discussion on issues that have been overlooked.

Name an Executor for your Will

Every will names an executor. The executor's function is to become your personal representative to look after all legal matters concerning the rights and obligations that you leave behind, and to carry out the wishes of your last will and testament.

If you have named an executor in your will **make sure that you have informed them** that you have done so. They are not forced by law to act as your executor and if they do accept the role, they need to be prepared.

Naming two or more persons as co-executors can lead to problems because it can create confusion and disagreement with respect to responsibilities. In some cases, the signatures of all co-executors may be required which can lead to frustrating delays with regard to settling estate matters.

Qualities of a Good Executor:
They have to be trustworthy with money. This means that the person has honesty, integrity, and a history of being responsible with financial matters. The person should have a fair chance of surviving you. It could be a close family member (spouse, child, or younger sibling), a good friend, neighbour, or business associate. These qualifications are mandatory for any executor, and any person that does not meet these criteria should not be your executor.

You should always name a second person as an **alternate executor**, in case your first named executor dies before you, is unable to act, or simply doesn't want to accept the appointment.

The person should be reasonably diligent and prudent. They do not have to have a high-end professional occupation but they should have the ability to recognize what they don't know and be willing to seek professional advice when they require it.

It is helpful (but not mandatory) if the person is geographically close to where you reside at your death, and preferably in Canada. When you die, all of your property becomes a trust, and your executor becomes a trustee of your assets. The location of the trust is the residence of the trustee, which can sometimes have adverse tax implications for your estate.

The person you name in your will as executor does not become your executor until you die, and the person accepts the appointment.

The Estate of the Deceased

The estate typically consists of any land, house, money, investment assets, personal items and other assets that the deceased owned.

Probate

Probate is the process of getting the courts to rule that the will is legally valid. The person who died and made the will is the testator.

Certain assets can be passed down without requiring probate. These assets by-pass the will and include joint bank accounts, jointly owned vehicles, and some other jointly owned assets. In addition, RRSP accounts, RRIF accounts, TFSA accounts, segregated funds and insurance policies where a beneficiary is named are not subject to probate. In these cases, a notarized copy of the death certificate is usually sufficient.

Duties of an Executor

While laws vary from one province to another, the overall duties of an executor in Canada are fairly consistent. The Canadian Bar Association, British Columbian Branch, has published a list of duties and posted them on their website at www.cba.org/BC/public_media/wills/178.aspx.

Before accepting the role of an executor, you should be aware of these duties. The list is extensive and includes the following:

- The executor is named in a will and gathers up the estate assets, pays the deceased's debts and divides what remains among the beneficiaries.

- You confirm that you are named as the executor by checking the original version of the will.

- You cannot be made to act as the executor but once you begin dealing with the process you are legally bound. It can be challenging, time consuming and stressful so make your decision carefully.

- If you accept the role of executor, consider hiring a lawyer to help with the paperwork and advise you of your obligations. The estate is responsible for the lawyer's fees.

- You are responsible for making the funeral arrangements but you will want to consider the wishes of the deceased and their family.

- Confirm that the will is the deceased's last will by checking with the Vital Statistics Agency. Most lawyers send a wills notice to Vital Statistics for every will they prepare.

- Cancel all the deceased person's charge cards and subscriptions. Ensure that the estate is protected and that sufficient insurance is in place. Valuables should be stored safely and unoccupied dwellings should have the locks changed immediately.

- Immediately notify all potential beneficiaries by giving them written notice and a copy of the will. This is typically done by the estate's lawyer.

- Prepare and submit the necessary probate documents to the court. You will have to pay the probate fees assessed by the court registry on behalf of the estate.

- If the estate includes investment securities such as stocks, bonds and mutual funds, you may have to apply for probate to transfer them.

- If applicable, notify the Canada Pension Plan and Old Age Security offices of the death. Apply for any survivor and death benefits that may be available. Check for any employer pensions and benefits the deceased may have had.

- File the necessary income tax returns and pay income tax as required from the assets of the estate. Obtain a tax clearance certificate from the Canada Revenue Agency that confirms all income taxes have been paid.

- Pay the estate's debts before you distribute the estate. You could be held personally liable if you fail to do so. Consulting a lawyer is a good idea.

- Submit a full accounting of the estate's financial activities and obtain a release from each beneficiary and then distribute the remaining assets as directed in the will.

Executor Compensation

Executors are entitled to compensation for the work that they do for the administration of an estate. This compensation is over and above any costs incurred by the executor.

An expected range of compensation often falls between 1% and 5% of the total value of the estate. The appropriate amount will depend on the complexity of the estate, the amount of responsibility assumed by the executor, the amount of time required and other factors.

Trust companies can be named as the executor of an estate and, in that case, the level of compensation should be outlined in the will. In fact, it is probably a good idea to outline compensation, regardless of who the executor may be.

Being an executor isn't easy. There's plenty of paperwork to be done, lots of interaction with government agencies, registries and lawyers. There are always beneficiaries putting on pressure to do things more quickly. And if all of that weren't tough enough, an executor **risks personal liability** for any mistakes he or she makes.

Five common mistakes executors can make:

- Ignoring inconvenient or unpopular parts of the will.
- Failing to communicate with the beneficiaries.
- Ignoring the limits of their role and using estate funds inappropriately.
- Failing to pay debts and taxes before paying the beneficiaries.
- Trying to do things cheaply by failing to use professional help.

NOTES:

- Term insurance is the least expensive way to purchase a substantial death benefit.
- Permanent insurance can have a tax deferred savings feature.
- Two common permanent insurance policies are whole life insurance and universal life insurance.
- Two types of insurance that you should strongly consider are long term disability insurance and life insurance if you have dependents who rely on your income.
- Three types of insurance you don't need are life insurance for children, mortgage life insurance and RRSP insurance.
- You may want to consider critical illness insurance or long term care insurance depending upon your situation and the cost of the insurance.
- Carefully consider your choice of executor and be sure to inform them that you have chosen them.
- Life insurance is only one aspect of estate planning. Complete an estate planning checklist to ensure that all is in order.
- You do not have to accept the role as executor, but if you do, you need to understand your responsibilities.

SECTION SIX

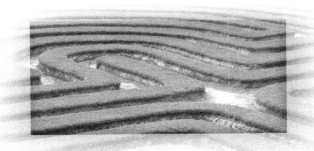

ADMINISTRATION AND PAPERWORK

CHOOSING AN ADVISOR

ONCE YOU HAVE decided to make a commitment to planning and saving for retirement, the next decision should be whether you want to tackle this project on your own or if you want to enlist the services of a financial advisor. Each of us has to decide which course of action best suits our needs.

DO IT YOURSELF

The biggest advantage to tackling your personal finances without enlisting the services of a financial advisor is that you will probably save on fees. However, if you decide to go down this route, there is a huge leap from theory to reality.

In the beginning, setting up financial goals, implementing an investment plan and following the markets can be exciting. But investing can be hard work and, like any other task, it becomes tedious for many. Interest can wane and important issues can be overlooked or ignored.

Other issues must be considered.

If you have a spouse, the decision should be made together. While one partner may enjoy working with finances and managing money, the other may not. What happens if the person who manages the family finances can no longer do so?

If a relationship has been established with an advisor, it becomes an easy transition; if not, important decisions need to be made and sometimes at short notice. At the very least, the partner who does not enjoy managing their personal finances alone should establish an account and build a relationship with an advisor. The partner who does enjoy the challenge can continue to do so on their own.

Of course, there will always be stories of investors who dumped their advisor at the bottom of the market and never looked back. The chances are if they had been doing it on their own, they would have suffered a similar setback, followed by a similar rebound. Such anecdotal stories are like the markets themselves... timing is everything.

These kinds of examples are anecdotal evidence not based on research. Still, they resonate with us because they appeal to our emotions, particularly after a period of less than stellar market returns.

The Advisor Advantage

However, there is information available that is based on research rather than on somewhat unique stories of failure and success.

The Investment Funds Institute of Canada published a paper titled "The Value of Financial Advice" that used data compiled by Ipsos Reid. It identifies many of these issues and a compelling argument is made for employing the services of a financial advisor.

It was discovered that in every income category individuals who used an advisor had accumulated significantly more investment assets. The same discrepancy existed when individuals were categorized by age rather than income.

The study found that advisors provided valuable guidance in helping their clients choose an appropriate asset mix for their circumstances, a critical factor for achieving success.

It also provided a word of caution.

Though investors are often coaxed by widespread media commentary that they can do better on their own through low or no advice embedded products, such as exchange-traded funds, the reality is that the investment decisions of investors, without advice, are very often driven by short-term biases. Investors often cycle between being over-cautious and under-cautious, and very often at precisely the wrong times.

The full report can be seen at www.ific.ca/Content/Document.aspx?id=5906.

There are those who are ready and willing to tackle their personal finances on their own. It is less expensive than using a financial advisor but their support network is much more limited. Another consideration is the value of personal time spent on planning and investing. Is it time well spent or is it taking away from your productive working time or your enjoyable recreation time?

You should take all of these factors into consideration before making your decision of whether to employ the services of a financial advisor.

Choosing a Financial Advisor

By now you have a good idea of the entire investment process. However, it is one thing to know what to expect when you walk into a financial advisor's office; it is another thing to find an advisor that suits your needs.

The truth is that the same investors who are unprepared or uninterested in handling their personal finances are probably equally unprepared for the task of choosing a financial advisor. There are many great financial advisors but not every one of them will suit your needs.

Multiple Advisors

One school of thought is to use more than one advisor in order to achieve a diversified approach to managing your money. This approach is less efficient than most people realize and can actually do more harm than good.

When managing your personal finances, there are many factors to consider. It is somewhat like putting the pieces of a jigsaw puzzle together. Now imagine that the pieces of this jigsaw puzzle are scattered among three different offices with three different people trying to imagine what the finished picture should look like. Without knowing whether or not they have the pieces they need, assembling that puzzle would be difficult, if not impossible.

The same applies to your personal finances. Using multiple advisors can lead to overlap and gaps in your investment portfolio as one advisor does not know what the other is doing. It can also lead to incomplete financial plans, the creation of unwanted tax liabilities and overlooked estate planning issues.

Rather than improving your diversification and returns, you run the risk of accomplishing the opposite.

Choosing the right advisor
The alternative is to do your homework ahead of time and find an advisor who suits your needs. The following guidelines can help you make that choice.

Choosing the individual is more important than choosing the firm. The challenge is in finding someone you are comfortable with who can also offer the products and services you require.

It is estimated that there are over 50,000 financial advisors in Canada, including accountants, lawyers and perhaps even your local banker. How do you know which one is right for you?

Trust is critical. A large part of your retirement lifestyle is going to be guided by investment income rather than Canada Pension Plan and Old Age Security cheques. When choosing a financial advisor, find somebody who is willing to listen to your concerns, who demonstrates they understand your personal goals and financial situation, and who you feel good working with.

A good practice is to interview at least two or three financial advisors before making a choice. Here are some things to look for:

Advice
Advice involves more than just choosing investments. It can include financial planning advice, the types of accounts that should be opened,

help with pension plan questions and help with consolidating accounts. Investors who are comfortable doing all of that for themselves might be well suited to a discount broker or an online broker. Those who want personalized service and help in those areas and others should work with a full service investment dealer.

Products

Advisors who can offer a full range of products rather than just one type of product, such as a mutual fund, may be more objective with advice on which product best suits the client. A full service investment dealer can offer individual securities such as stocks, bonds and GICs as well as mutual funds and exchange traded funds. They have a far larger menu from which to choose.

Some advisors may work for firms that sell only products promoted by their firm. Advisors who sell only proprietary products are at a disadvantage because it is far more difficult for them to be objective.

Performance

Red flags should go up if an advisor promises better performance than his competitors or if he suggests that he can beat the market. If it could be done, the advisor wouldn't need a client base; he could simply invest his own money and become wealthy.

Credentials

An advisor and his firm must have the appropriate credentials.

There are a number of organizations that are involved in the education and oversight of advisors and their firms. One is the **Investment Industry Regulatory Organization of Canada** or IIROC. There are others as well, such as the **Mutual Fund Dealers Association of Canada** or MFDA. Investors should know the organization in which their investment firm holds a membership.

The website for IIROC is www.iiroc.ca.

The website for the MFDA is www.mfda.ca.

Advisors must also be licensed. IIROC advisors are licensed to sell individual securities, exchange traded funds and mutual funds with additional licenses available for options trading. MFDA advisors are licensed to sell mutual funds. Trading in commodities requires the advisor to hold a specialized commodities license.

In addition to being licensed to sell products, advisors may carry additional designations, such as CFP (chartered financial planner), CIM (Canadian investment manager), CFA (chartered financial analyst) and so on. While these designations indicate that an advisor has completed the required course work, it is not a guarantee they will suit your needs. It is only one of many factors to be considered.

The other problem with designations is that there are a multitude of them. Every organization tries to promote its designation as the industry standard but in reality there is no one designation that stands above the rest.

In the accounting profession, the designation CA tells everyone in the world that the individual is a chartered accountant. In the engineering profession the professional designation is P Eng. There is no overall equivalent designation in the financial services industry.

Experience and History

Investors should check the resume of a potential advisor. In addition to education and credentials, the employment history of a financial advisor should be examined. If the advisor has a history of frequently changing firms, there may be a legitimate reason but it would be wise to investigate further.

Compensation

While you shouldn't expect a financial advisor to disclose their level of income, it is worth asking them *how* they are compensated. If the advisor is forthcoming about his method of compensation and willingly discusses how he is paid on a variety of different products and services, it is a good sign. On the other hand, if the advisor is reluctant to discuss compensation, the relationship is not getting off to a good start.

Communication

Another factor is the preferred method of communication used by the advisor. It they rely heavily on email but you prefer frequent face-to-face meetings, it may not be the best fit. Because the financial services industry relies heavily on communication, it is a good idea for clients and advisors to be on the same page.

Business Style

Some advisors have a business based on active trading, while others take a longer term approach and focus on portfolio management. Know what kind of a financial advisor you want and don't hesitate to ask a potential advisor what the focus of their business is. It is rare that an advisor can be all things to all people. Be wary of those who think they can. Choose one whose business style best suits your needs.

Support

Most financial advisors work with an administrative assistant. When interviewing an advisor it is a good idea to ask to meet the assistant. At the same time, discuss what role the assistant will play and what role the advisor will play in managing your account.

Many questions, such as requests for a cheque, information about tax receipts or updates on documentation are often handled by the assistant. Because they are part of the team, learn who they are and what their role is. It will form part of your decision.

Friends, colleagues and relatives

If you are aware of someone who deals with a financial advisor, don't just ask their opinion; ask specific questions. They may be able to provide some insight that can help you make a decision.

Gut Feeling

Sometimes a first impression goes a long way. If the advisor's approach makes you feel uncomfortable, the chances are that feeling won't go away. In this case, it might be to everyone's advantage to walk away from a situation before a relationship even begins.

Finding a firm

Canadian Securities Administrators has an excellent website (www.securities-administrators.ca) that provides links and information on a host of investment related issues, including finding and working with a financial advisor.

In addition, a list of firms that belong to the Investment Industry Regulatory Organization of Canada can be found on their website at: http://www.iiroc.ca/industry/industrycompliance/Documents/PeerGroupList_en.pdf. Many of the firms will have websites indicating the location of their nearest office. You can also check the yellow pages at www.canada411.ca/ to see which firms have offices in close proximity to where you live.

Similarly, Mutual Fund Dealers Association (MFDA) firms can be checked at: http://www.mfda.ca/members/members.html.

NOTES:

Choosing an investment advisor is an important decision and several factors should be considered. A checklist may include:

- What kind of advice does the advisor provide?
- What investment and insurance products are available through the advisor?
- What kind of performance promises does the advisor make?
- What are the advisor's credentials?
- How much experience does the advisor have?
- Is the advisor willing to discuss how he is compensated?
- How does the advisor communicate with his clients?
- What kind of approach does the advisor take when managing portfolios? Does that approach fit with your needs?
- Who provides the administrative support for the advisor?
- Who do your friends, relatives and colleagues suggest might be a good advisor?
- What is your gut feeling when you meet with the advisor?

ESTABLISH YOUR ACCOUNTS

There are a wide range of choices available to investors when it comes time to open an account and begin putting the investment plan into action. The three main categories are taxable investment accounts, tax-deferred investment accounts and tax-free investment accounts.

When you open an account with an IIROC firm, you can add new investments, transfer investments from other financial institutions and consolidate your holdings without going through the process of opening new accounts. It is simple and efficient.

- One major advantage is the convenience of holding your investments in one place.
- Another is that your financial advisor can clearly see the big picture and provide you with guidance that would otherwise be difficult should your investments be scattered among various financial institutions.

Don't underestimate the value of these benefits.

Taxable Investment Accounts

The main feature of these accounts is that dividends and interest are taxed on an ongoing basis. Capital gains are taxed when a profit is realized on the sale of an investment.

Taxable investment accounts are the least efficient of all accounts simply because of the tax treatment they receive. As such, they should be considered as a vehicle for long term savings only after tax-deferred and tax-free accounts have been maximized.

There can be three types of growth within a taxable investment account, including interest, dividends and capital gains. Each of these is taxed at a different rate with interest being subject to the highest tax rate. In other words, a 4% return on a GIC may not be as good as a 4% return on a mutual fund, stock or ETF when taxes are taken into consideration. Since after-tax growth is the only growth an investor gets to keep, taxation is an important factor in making investment decisions in a taxable account.

If you are not comfortable choosing investments that will maximize your after-tax return, you may want to seek input from your financial advisor.

A taxable investment account that is part of a long term retirement plan should be considered as part of a total investment package along with an RRSP account and a TFSA account. By considering all three accounts, a financial advisor can help you allocate investments among these three accounts to create the most tax efficient growth.

Over time, these small advantages can add up and make a difference.

Even if you have a long term focus, you may believe that you have found a short term trading opportunity or a "can't miss" stock pick. It can be equated to impulse buying when a shopper sees something in a store that they 'have to have' because it is on sale and too good to pass up. In most cases, these investments don't fit within the guidelines of the long term plan that has been established but the opportunity is still appealing.

There is a solution to this dilemma.

You can choose to open a separate trading account that is designated for these types of investments. It would be deemed to be a high risk account and should be limited to investment capital not required for your long term retirement plan. In other words, it should be money that you can afford to lose without having it affect your retirement plans.

It is a topic you should think about and discuss with your advisor.

Tax Deferred Accounts

In Canada the term RRSP has become synonymous with saving for retirement. Nevertheless, misconceptions still exist and, despite powerful tax incentives, the average Canadian still does not take full advantage of Registered Retirement Savings Plans.

The tax incentives are twofold. The first incentive is the tax credit an investor receives when the contribution is made. The second incentive is that the investments can grow inside the account without being taxed.

At some point in the future the money has to be withdrawn from an RRSP account and it is taxed at that time. In other words, the tax is deferred until the money is withdrawn, rather than on a year-by-year basis.

The misconception about an RRSP is that it is an investment; it is not. An RRSP is simply an account that can hold a wide variety of investments where the growth on those investments is not taxed.

Banks will often offer an RRSP that can hold only one investment that is typically a term deposit that pays a specific rate of interest. That has led to some confusion that RRSPs are an investment. An RRSP, however, is an account rather than investment and, depending upon the financial institution that you deal with, the investments that can be held in that account are virtually unlimited.

Canadians can contribute up to 18% of earned income each year to an RRSP account and unused contributions can be carried forward. There is a maximum contribution limit which was $22,450 in 2011 but you would have to earn over $125,000 per year to reach that maximum. With the average contribution in 2009 at about $2700, it is clear that the average Canadian has not been taking full advantage of their RRSP contribution limits.

There is a caveat to RRSP contribution limits. Investors who are members of an employee sponsored pension plan will have their contribution limits reduced.

In the past, investors had to wait for their T4 slips in order to calculate their RRSP contribution room and because these were usually issued in late January, it resulted in a short time frame for investors to calculate their contribution room and make the deposit to their RRSP accounts. Contribution room is now calculated on the PREVIOUS year's income and it is now included on the taxpayer's notice of assessment, which usually arrives in May or June.

If you have the funds available, there is no reason to wait until February to make your contribution when you have been given the exact amount of your contribution room six months or eight months before the March 1st deadline for contributions.

The RRSP is an account designed to help you accumulate savings for retirement. Upon retirement, the account can be converted to a Registered Retirement Income Fund (RRIF) account from which you can withdraw these accumulated savings on a regular basis. In many cases, the investments don't need to be changed when an RRSP is converted to a RRIF.

There are a couple of key points to remember about RRSPs and RRIFs.

An RRSP must be collapsed during the year in which you turn 71 and at that time you have three primary choices:

- The entire amount can be withdrawn and the tax paid on that amount.
- The investments in the RRSP can be sold and the proceeds used to purchase an annuity.
- Or the account can be converted to a RRIF and the amounts can be withdrawn on a regular basis throughout retirement, subject to a minimum amount each year.

Of course, you don't have to wait until age 71 as these same choices are available to you prior to that time.

After age 65, the first $2000 of pension income and/or RRIF income each year is tax free. When you combine the benefits of the tax credit upon contribution, the tax-free growth and the fact that the first $2000 of income each year is tax-free, the case for RRSPs is compelling.

Tax-Free Accounts

If there was any doubt the Federal Government wanted Canadians to take more personal responsibility for their retirement savings, then the introduction of the Tax-Free Savings Account or the TFSA should erase that doubt. It is important to know that a TFSA is an account that can hold a variety of investments, rather than an investment itself. The investment options are typically the same as for an RRSP.

As with any new product or service, investors are still feeling their way around TFSAs and how they should be used. Make no mistake; these are a great vehicle for those who want to save for retirement. Over time they could make taxable savings accounts almost irrelevant for a lot of Canadians.

While there is no tax benefit in making the contribution, the growth in the account is tax-free. Unlike RRSP accounts or RRIF accounts, there is no tax paid when funds are withdrawn from the account. It gets better. Funds can be withdrawn from the account and then be re-contributed in the next calendar year. This is in complete contrast to an RRSP where once funds are withdrawn they cannot be replaced unless the investor has sufficient contribution room.

Another benefit of the TFSA that differentiates it from RRSP accounts is that contributions can continue to be made after age 71. Every year another $5500 can be moved from a taxable account to a TFSA account which can mean more tax-free income for a retiree.

As with an RRSP, there is the misconception that a TFSA is an investment. These are not investments; they are accounts which can hold any number of investments. No one can 'buy' a TFSA or an RRSP. They can make a contribution to that account and then an investment can be chosen.

Amazingly, TFSA accounts have been opened and the deposits left in daily interest savings that pay less than 0.5% per year. The whole idea of a tax-free savings account is to protect your growth from taxes. If there is no growth, there is no need for a tax-free savings account and 0.5% comes pretty close to no growth.

Investors need to seriously explore all options available to them for their TFSA accounts.

THE MONEY MAZE AND YOUR PATH TO SUCCESS

Taxable Account Growth					TFSA Account Growth		
value	growth	taxes	net growth	Total	value	growth	Total
$5,000.00	$300.00	$99.00	$201.00	$5,201.00	$5,000.00	$300.00	$5,300.00
$10,201.00	$612.06	$201.98	$410.08	$10,611.08	$10,300.00	$618.00	$10,918.00
$15,611.08	$936.66	$309.10	$627.57	$16,238.65	$15,918.00	$955.08	$16,873.08
$21,238.65	$1,274.32	$420.53	$853.79	$22,092.44	$21,873.08	$1,312.38	$23,185.46
$27,092.44	$1,625.55	$536.43	$1,089.12	$28,181.56	$28,185.46	$1,691.13	$29,876.59
$33,181.56	$1,990.89	$656.99	$1,333.90	$34,515.45	$34,876.59	$2,092.60	$36,969.19
$39,515.45	$2,370.93	$782.41	$1,588.52	$41,103.97	$41,969.19	$2,518.15	$44,487.34
$46,103.97	$2,766.24	$912.86	$1,853.38	$47,957.35	$49,487.34	$2,969.24	$52,456.58
$52,957.35	$3,177.44	$1,048.56	$2,128.89	$55,086.24	$57,456.58	$3,447.39	$60,903.97
$60,086.24	$3,605.17	$1,189.71	$2,415.47	$62,501.71	$65,903.97	$3,954.24	$69,858.21
$67,501.71	$4,050.10	$1,336.53	$2,713.57	$70,215.28	$74,858.21	$4,491.49	$79,349.71
$75,215.28	$4,512.92	$1,489.26	$3,023.65	$78,238.93	$84,349.71	$5,060.98	$89,410.69
$83,238.93	$4,994.34	$1,648.13	$3,346.20	$86,585.14	$94,410.69	$5,664.64	$100,075.33
$91,585.14	$5,495.11	$1,813.39	$3,681.72	$95,266.86	$105,075.33	$6,304.52	$111,379.85
$100,266.86	$6,016.01	$1,985.28	$4,030.73	$104,297.59	$116,379.85	$6,982.79	$123,362.64
$109,297.59	$6,557.86	$2,164.09	$4,393.76	$113,691.35	$128,362.64	$7,701.76	$136,064.40
$118,691.35	$7,121.48	$2,350.09	$4,771.39	$123,462.74	$141,064.40	$8,463.86	$149,528.26
$128,462.74	$7,707.76	$2,543.56	$5,164.20	$133,626.94	$154,528.26	$9,271.70	$163,799.96
$138,626.94	$8,317.62	$2,744.81	$5,572.80	$144,199.75	$168,799.96	$10,128.00	$178,927.96
$149,199.75	$8,951.98	$2,954.15	$5,997.83	$155,197.58	$183,927.96	$11,035.68	$194,963.63
$160,197.58	$9,611.85	$3,171.91	$6,439.94	$166,637.52	$199,963.63	$11,997.82	$211,961.45
$171,637.52	$10,298.25	$3,398.42	$6,899.83	$178,537.35	$216,961.45	$13,017.69	$229,979.14
$183,537.35	$11,012.24	$3,634.04	$7,378.20	$190,915.55	$234,979.14	$14,098.75	$249,077.89
$195,915.55	$11,754.93	$3,879.13	$7,875.81	$203,791.35	$254,077.89	$15,244.67	$269,322.56
Taxable Account Income					TFSA Account Income		
Value	Income	Tax	Net Income		Value	Net Income	
$203,791.35	$12,227.48	$4,035.07	$8,192.41		$269,322.56	$16,159.35	

Specialty Accounts

A Registered Education Savings Plan (RESP) is a specialty account that allows for tax-free growth within the account with the withdrawals taxed in the hands of the beneficiary. There are government grants available for RESPs and withdrawals are subject to specific conditions.

While they provide an excellent way to save for the costs of post-secondary education, you need to be aware of the nuances unique to RESP accounts. It is a good topic to discuss with your financial advisor.

A Registered Disability Savings Plan (RDSP) is a specialty plan designed "to help parents and others save for the long-term financial security of a person who is eligible for the disability tax credit". Information on contribution limits, payments, grants and information on other regulations applicable to RDSP accounts can be seen on the Canada Revenue Agency website.

The direct link is http://www.cra-arc.gc.ca/tx/ndvdls/tpcs/rdsp-reei/menu-eng.html.

The Home Buyer's Plan and the Lifelong Learning Plan are provisions that allow you, under special circumstances, to withdraw funds from your RRSP tax-free. However, those withdrawals have to be repaid to your RRSP over time. You can consult with your financial advisor for more information.

Defined Contribution Pension Plans

Investors can often choose to consolidate their defined contribution pension assets with their financial advisor upon retirement. Once transferred, the investor can make the appropriate investment choices in consultation with their advisor.

The account is treated in a similar manner to an RRIF account. Growth is tax-free while the funds remain in the plan and any withdrawals from the plan are taxed at your marginal tax rate. Depending on the pension plan that originally managed the funds, there can be varying degrees of limitations on the withdrawals.

While the process is straightforward, the paperwork can be intimidating. It needs to be done correctly or the transfer will be rejected. That can mean re-submitting the appropriate documents with the corrections made.

There are several forms that are unique to pension accounts and transfers. In addition, a pension plan may have its own unique requirements.

Full service investment firms are aware of most of these quirks or will take the time to find out what is required, making the transition as smooth as possible for you.

Notes:

- Three general categories of accounts are taxable investment accounts, tax deferred accounts (RRSPs and RRIFs) and tax-free accounts (TFSAs).

- Specialty accounts include Registered Educational Savings Plans (RESPs) and Registered Disability Savings Plans (RDSPs).

- Defined contribution pension plans must be converted to an annuity or to a tax deferred account similar to a RRIF by age 71.

DOCUMENTATION

It used to be that business deals could be consummated with not much more than a handshake. Times have changed. The documentation now required to open an investment account can be overwhelming but investment dealers and financial advisors have to work within a strict code of conduct outlined by their professional organizations and mandated by both federal and provincial law.

That was a mouthful, but it gives you an idea of the new world of regulation that we live in today.

New investors are often surprised by the requirements and can show up unprepared. A quick view of what you can expect if you decide to open an account can help avoid these unexpected surprises. Being well prepared can help make the process run more smoothly.

Once your account documentation is complete and your accounts are established, transactions can be processed quickly and easily.

Required Information

You can expect the following information will be required when opening an account. Your advisor will appreciate it if you complete the account information form and bring it to your first meeting.

- Personal information
  - Name, address, telephone number, birthdate(s), social insurance number(s)
- Employment information
  - Name, address, occupation(s), years of service
- Family information
  - Marital status, dependents
- Financial information
  - Income, net worth, bank information
- Investment information
  - Investment experience, investment objectives, tolerance to risk, time horizon
- Supporting documents
  - Void cheque, valid picture ID (driver's license or passport, for example)

The account application form will have a section that asks the client for investment objectives and tolerance to risk. It might be the most important section of the form, yet it is poorly understood. Discussing this topic with your advisor can help clarify the picture for both of you.

A risk tolerance questionnaire is a good way for investors to help determine their profile.

Additional Information

Any additional material and information can be very helpful in interpreting your financial situation. While some of it may not apply to your situation, the more information that you can provide, the better. The list includes:

- Current statements of your existing investments including RRSP, RRIF, TFSA and taxable investment accounts.
- Your latest T4 or tax return.

- Your latest Notice of Assessment from the Canada Revenue Agency (CRA).
- A copy of your will and enduring power of attorney if you have one.
- Any employer pension plan information.
- Contact information for your lawyer and accountant.
- Social Insurance Numbers for any beneficiaries that will be named on your accounts.

Some of the information in the application form is required by the investment firm, some by IIROC (the Investment Industry Regulatory Organization of Canada) and some by Federal government regulations with regard to anti-money laundering initiatives. It is the world we live in today.

Any deficiencies in the information can result in an account not being approved and it would likely not be opened until that information is provided. This is frustrating for both the advisor and the client. The last thing an advisor wants to do is chase down missing information and the last thing a client wants is numerous phone calls and emails requesting additional information.

Doing a thorough, accurate job from the start also helps to get the relationship off to a good start.

All of this documentation comes from the golden rule of investment firms: Know Your Client. It helps to ensure that your investments are being managed to meet your needs while remaining compliant with industry and government regulations.

Updates Required

Every two or three years the information on your account needs to be verified to ensure it is still accurate and that it reflects your personal circumstances. It is also part of the 'Know Your Client' rule mandated by industry regulators. They want to ensure that the advisor is keenly aware of the client's circumstances because any recommendations made to the client are based on that information.

It can happen that clients will overlook the task of completing the updates and forms can be forgotten. When that situation occurs the hands of the advisor are tied. Accounts can be frozen with regard to making changes other than selling investments and issuing cheques.

Updates can be aggravating for both the client and the advisor but in the end they are designed to help protect the interests of the client and are a requirement that needs to be fulfilled.

Consolidating Accounts – Transfers from Other Institutions

The advantage of dealing with a full service investment dealer is that you can usually consolidate investments that you hold elsewhere into your new account. For example, you can hold all of your mutual funds, individual stocks, exchange traded funds, bonds and GICs in a single account. Each month you get one envelope and one statement that lists everything. In many cases, you can forego printed statements and apply for online access to your account.

Many investors are unsure about consolidating. First of all, they don't want to alienate the other advisors they are dealing with. Secondly, they may like to spread their investments around in an effort to diversify or perhaps determine who provides the best returns. And finally, they don't want to be paying a lot of fees, penalties and taxes to consolidate. If they had to do it all over again, they might do it differently, but since they started down this path, they are hesitant to change.

Each of these concerns should be addressed.

As an investor, you need to put your interests first. If that means staying where you are, that is what you should do, but if your interests are better served by consolidating your investments with one advisor, then that is what you should do. It should be treated as a business decision because that is what it is.

With regard to diversification, you probably have a better chance of getting the proper diversification by choosing one advisor and building a portfolio of quality investments with appropriate asset allocation where the various investments are complementing each other. When you are dealing with multiple advisors, the chances are that the left hand doesn't know what the right hand is doing. There could be gaps in some parts of the portfolio and improper concentration of investments in other parts of the portfolio. By choosing only one advisor, you will make your life simpler and your advisor will likely be able to do a better job.

As far as penalties and taxes go, there should be none. The *receiving institution* will usually pay the transfer in fees. It is a cost of acquiring new business. If they don't, you may want to question the value they place on your business.

Investors can usually transfer most of their investments 'in kind', which means you aren't selling them and re-buying; you are simply moving them from one account to another. It is usually a good idea to transfer 'in kind' whenever possible. When you transfer your investments in kind, there will be no commissions or redemption charges.

When it comes to taxes, even in the case of transferring accounts like RRSPs, you aren't withdrawing money from your account; you are only moving from one RRSP account to another. It is a 'tax sheltered' transfer.

As you can see, there are very few barriers to consolidating investments with a single advisor. The reasons people don't consolidate can be because they have existing relationships, they are unaware they can consolidate, they worry about the costs of making the move or they just don't get around to it.

The biggest misconception is that their money is safer if it is spread among a variety of institutions. In many cases that approach can result in poorer performance and higher volatility because of improper diversification.

The question of Canada Deposit Insurance Corporation (CDIC) coverage also comes up. The fact is that you can hold investments that qualify for CDIC coverage from a variety of issuers within your account at a full service investment dealer. Each of these would qualify for the maximum coverage available which is currently $100,000 per issuer. In other words, you could hold several hundred thousand dollars of GICs with your investment dealer and they could all be covered by CDIC. You would reap the benefits of safety and convenience in one package.

Each investor has to do what they feel is right for their own situation. For some, it is consolidating, for others it is dealing with multiple advisors.

There is no right way and no wrong way. Investors have to weigh the pros and cons then decide what the most important factors are.

Pension Plan Transfers

From time to time individuals will change careers and the circumstance can arise where they had a pension plan with their former employer. In many cases, the employee can take control of those pension assets by having them transferred into a Locked-In Retirement Account (LIRA) or a Locked-in RRSP (LRRSP) at an investment dealer.

LIRAs and locked-in RRSPs are similar to RRSPs in many ways. Your financial advisor can explain the differences in more detail but it is important to know the options that are available.

One advantage of holding a LIRA with your financial advisor, rather than leaving your assets in the pension plan, is convenience. With all of your investments in one place, it becomes easier to monitor your overall financial holdings.

Another advantage is that you can more easily ensure that the combined asset mix of your LIRA and the remainder of your personal investments are appropriate for your circumstances. When two portfolios (your pension and your personal investments) are managed in isolation of one another, there can be gaps or overlaps in the portfolios that make the overall investment mix inefficient.

Before you decide whether consolidation is appropriate, it is important to differentiate between the two types of pension plans. These differences were covered before, but they are worth repeating when it comes to the issue of consolidating your investment assets.

The first is a **defined benefit pension plan** which provides you with a guaranteed income for as long as you live. Keeping any defined benefit pension plans in place is often the preferable choice unless there are exceptional circumstances.

The second is a **defined contribution plan** which is a pool of money that provides no guaranteed income upon retirement. These pensions can often be left where they are if you change employers but since these are not guaranteed pensions there are fewer reasons to leave them in place. In order to manage your finances more efficiently it can make sense to consolidate these plans with your investment dealer.

Transferring those pension assets when the opportunity presents itself is an option that should be carefully considered.

Reading your statements

When you begin an investment program with the firm of your choice, you will begin to receive statements usually at least once a quarter and often on a monthly basis. They are more complex than bank statements and include a great deal of information in addition to the value of your investments.

Some of this information may include the adjusted cost base of each investment, the asset mix, contributions made to the account, withdrawals taken from the account, dividends and interest collected, account activity with respect to purchases and sales of investments, changes in the value of the account over the reporting periods and so on.

If you have never had an investment account, it is a good idea to schedule an appointment with your financial advisor once you have received your first statement. The two of you can go through the details line by line. It can help you identify some of the key information and understand how that information is reported.

Maintain realistic expectations; investment accounts are not bank accounts. Don't expect your portfolio to gain value immediately. It will rise and fall in value, sometimes for periods longer than expected and the growth will not be steady month after month.

Keep in mind that while your money is usually accessible, it is not usually instantly accessible. Investments have to be sold, the transfer of ownership processed by the transfer agent and the funds released. These funds then have to be delivered by cheque or by direct deposit to your bank account. When requesting a withdrawal from your account you should count on at least five business days before receiving the proceeds.

THE ROLE OF THE ADMINISTRATIVE ASSISTANT

While the exact role of the administrative assistant may vary from one advisor to the next, they serve a very important role in the management of your portfolio. Some of their duties may include:

- Ensuring your account documentation is completed properly.
- Processing requests for cheques or withdrawals from your account.
- Setting up your RRIF withdrawal schedule.
- Inquiring about the status of any transfers.
- Checking on dividend re-investments.
- Providing updates on tax receipts, RRSP contribution receipts and capital gains that must be claimed on tax returns.

The time consuming burden of these tasks falls on their shoulders and frees up time for the financial advisor to review your accounts, research investments, prepare retirement plans and make investment recommendations.

Learning how your advisor and their assistant divide up the responsibilities associated with managing your account can help make everything run more smoothly and efficiently. Ask your advisor if they have a checklist of who is responsible for the various functions of the investment team. It can save time and reduce misunderstandings.

NOTES:

- Government and financial industry regulation requires that significant information is gathered before an investment account can be opened.
- Governments require information to assist in their efforts to prevent illegal activity such as money laundering and fraud.
- Industry regulators need to understand your personal situation in order to monitor the efforts of financial advisors to ensure they are acting in your best interest.
- It is a requirement that your account information is updated every two to three years.
- Accounts from several different firms can often be consolidated with one financial advisor by completing a simple account transfer form.
- Upon changing employers or upon retirement, your pension plan can often be transferred into an account managed by your financial advisor.

FEES AND COMMISSIONS

Unfortunately, there is nothing straightforward about the fees and commissions on investment products.

The financial services industry has done itself a disservice in the way that fees and commissions are disclosed. Many investors may be unaware that they are paying anything when in reality they may be paying abnormally high fees. It is one part of the industry that needs to be more transparent and simplified.

Investors should try to ensure that they are reasonable. On the other hand, investors should not become obsessed with fees at the expense of making appropriate decisions. Reducing fees does not guarantee superior returns, nor does it ensure that the risk in your portfolio will be reduced. A well-constructed portfolio with moderate fees is far better than a poorly constructed portfolio with low fees.

Fees are an easy target but in reality they rank lower on the list in terms of what affects portfolio performance. Five factors that affect the rate of return you can expect to achieve include:

- Asset allocation.
- Cash flow into or out of the account.

- Security selection – choice of investments.
- Timing of changes made to asset allocation (see the Dalbar study discussed earlier).
- Fees and commissions.

The complex world of fees and commissions needs to be examined in more detail. It can be difficult to absorb all of the variations and it is a good idea to mark this section for reference if you have any questions.

Trading commissions are those charges that are incurred when a transaction, either a buy or a sell, is made. ***Management fees*** are those fees charged on an ongoing basis for as long as they are held in the investor's portfolio.

To further complicate matters, an investor can choose a fee-based account where there are no transaction fees and a management fee is charged on all products. Or they may choose a commission-based account where there is a trading commission but no management fee charged on some products but where a management fee may apply on other products.

If you aren't confused yet, you are doing well.

Individual investments such as bonds, common shares and preferred shares have **no management fee** associated with them. Investments that represent a basket of individual investments, such as mutual funds or exchange traded funds (ETFs) do have a ***management fee*** associated with constructing and managing the basket of investments on an ongoing basis. These fees are referred to as management expense ratios or MERs.

MANAGEMENT FEES FOR MUTUAL FUNDS AND ETFS

The following table provides some guidelines with respect to management fees on various products.

Fees and Commissions

Asset Class	ETF MERs Avg	Mutual Fund MERs			
		Low	Medium	High	Extreme
Canadian Government Bond	0.30%	1.00% or less	1.00% to 1.45%	1.45% to 1.70%	over 1.70%
Corporate Bond	0.45%	1.25% or less	1.25% to 1.65%	1.65% to 1.90%	over 1.90%
Global / High Yield Bond	0.55%	1.75% or less	1.75% to 2.00%	2.00% to 2.20%	over 2.20%
Emerging Markets Bond	0.60%	1.75% or less	1.75% to 2.00%	2.00% to 2.20%	over 2.20%
Canadian Large Cap Equity	0.25%	2.00% or less	2.00% to 2.35%	2.35% to 2.60%	over 2.60%
Canadian Small Cap Equity	0.60%	2.20% or less	2.20% to 2.60%	2.60% to 2.90%	over 2.90%
US Equity	0.25%	2.10% or less	2.10% to 2.45%	2.45% to 2.70%	over 2.70%
International Equity	0.45%	2.30% or less	2.30% to 2.65%	2.65% to 2.90%	over 2.90%
Emerging Markets / Special Equity	0.65%	2.50% or less	2.50% to 2.85%	2.85% to 3.10%	over 3.10%

COMMISSION BASED ACCOUNTS

Common shares, preferred shares and ETFs are all traded on stock exchanges and trading commissions will apply on a buy AND on a sell. These commissions will vary with the individual unit price, the total size of the transaction and the policy of the investment dealer. An annual management fee will also apply on ETFs but this charge is not seen on client statements. It can usually be checked on the website of the company that manages the ETF or the fund's prospectus.

The following table is an example of the approximate commissions an investor can expect to pay when buying or selling exchange traded investments. Exchange traded investments include individual investments such as stocks and broadly based investments such as exchange traded funds (ETFs).

Exchange Traded Commission Schedule

Greater of:

Share Price	Minimum Commission	Commission Rate
less than $1	$125	3.00%
$1 to $5	$125	2.75%
$5 to $10	$125	2.50%
$10 to $15	$125	2.25%
$15 to $20	$125	2.00%
$20 to $25	$125	1.75%
$25 to $50	$125	1.50%
over $50	$125	1.25%

There are a variety of sales charges (commissions) that can be applied on the purchase or sale of a mutual fund. These charges, if applicable, are in addition to the management expense that is applied on an ongoing basis. In summary, the various sales charge formats include:

No load – This commission is exactly as it sounds. There is no commission charged when you make the purchase and no commission or fees are applied if and when you sell the fund.

Front load – There can be a commission applied of up to 5% when a purchase is made but there are no fees or commissions applied upon the sale. In some cases, financial advisors will charge a commission of zero upon the purchase, in which case it is the equivalent of buying the fund with no load.

Low load – There is no commission applied when the purchase is

Fees and Commissions

made but a redemption fee will typically apply if the fund is sold within three years of purchase. If it is sold after that period, no redemption fee is charged. Each fund has a different holding period during which these redemption charges apply.

Deferred Sales Charge or Rear load – Similar to a low load, there is no commission applied when the purchase is made; however, the holding period can be as long as six or seven years before the redemption charges are eliminated. Funds cashed in before that time can have significant redemption charges, usually higher than the charges on a fund sold with a low load commission option.

With the low load or deferred sales charge option, investors can typically redeem up to 10% of their units each year without incurring a redemption charge.

This is where some of the transparency problems begin. Investors may be unaware or may fail to remember that these fees can apply on sales. They are listed in the fund prospectus but the document is long and the fee schedule is often overlooked or forgotten.

The following table provides an example of the fees that are applicable under the various sales charge formats for mutual funds. While the actual charges will vary from one mutual fund company to another, the information in this table is a good guideline.

Mutual Fund Redemption Schedule
(charges applicable on the sale of funds)

Year	Redemption Schedule						
	One	Two	Three	Four	Five	Six	Seven
Front Load Sales Charge	no redemption charges						
Low Load Sales Charge	3.00%	2.50%	2.00%	Nil	Nil	Nil	Nil
Deferred Sales Charge	6.00%	5.50%	5.00%	4.50%	4.00%	3.00%	Nil

Fee Based Accounts

With fee based accounts, investors are allowed a limited number of transactions without incurring any commissions. The number of trades is usually sufficient for any well managed portfolio. The trading limit makes this type of account impractical for day traders or very active traders.

The commission free trades apply to all exchange traded products such as common shares, preferred shares and ETFs as well as to mutual funds. In fact, a special class of mutual funds with a lower MER is available for fee based accounts. They were developed to ensure that investors weren't paying two management fees on the same product, one at the investment level and one on the account level.

Typically, an investor has a choice of a fee based account where a flat fee is charged, or one where the fee is higher on the equity portion of the account and lower on the fixed income portion of the account. Once again, the choices are confusing.

The following table is an example of management fees on fee based accounts where a flat fee is charged whether the investments are equities or bonds. Many investment dealers will also offer a tiered fee schedule and investors can inquire about the fee levels of each platform and decide whether either one of them meets their needs. It may be that a commission based account is more suitable.

Investors should inquire about the fees they will be expected to pay on fee based accounts. There may be a difference among firms and advisors may have some latitude in the level of fees their firms allow them to charge. There may be room for negotiation; it never hurts to ask.

Account Size	Management Fee		
	Low	Medium	High
$100K to $250K	1.25%	1.75%	2.25%
$250K to $500K	1.00%	1.50%	2.00%
$500K to $750K	0.75%	1.25%	1.75%
$750K to $1MM	0.65%	1.00%	1.25%
$1MM to $2MM	0.50%	0.75%	1.00%
Over $2MM	0.40%	0.65%	0.90%

A Hybrid Account

The commission and fee structures available to investors will continue to evolve. Perhaps a hybrid structure will emerge that would separate the charges for advice and for trading. Each account would be subject to a commission for each transaction. This commission would be substantially lower than what is charged in a traditional commission based account, while the ongoing fee applied to each account would be substantially lower than what is currently charged in a traditional fee based account.

When it comes to fees and commissions, investors need to be aware of what they are actually paying and what a reasonable amount is. The tables are meant to be a point of comparison for fees.

What about bonds?

While it may appear there are no commissions in bond transactions, it would be naïve to assume the process occurs without any form of compensation.

In order to understand this compensation, you need to take a closer look at how bonds are traded. Unlike stocks where there is a centralized exchange to facilitate transactions between buyers and sellers, there is no equivalent exchange for bonds.

Investment dealers have a 'bond desk' or bond department that carries an inventory of bonds. Bonds are offered to clients from that inventory and when a client wants to sell a bond, the dealer buys it and adds it to their inventory. It is not typically an exchange between two investors, as with stocks; it is a purchase from the dealer or a sale to the dealer.

This background will help you understand how commissions on bonds are charged.

But before talking about commissions, the pricing on bonds needs to be explained. Once again, it may not seem straightforward to the average investor. Bonds are traded in multiples of $1000 face value but the price is based on a base of 100, otherwise referred to as par. A $10,000 bond trading at 100 would cost $10,000 not $1 million dollars. If the same bond was trading at 95, the value would be $9,500.

It is confusing for many people; however, it is worthwhile information. The following example illustrates this point:

> An investor buys a bond with a face value of $10,000 and pays 99.50 for a total cost of $9950. The dealer may have purchased that bond earlier for 98.50 or a total cost of $9850 and held it in their inventory. The commission or profit on the trade for the dealer, in this case, was $100. The $100 never shows up as a commission but it is embedded in the price.
>
> The investor receives their bond knowing full well what it will be worth at maturity and how much interest it will generate over that period of time. Upon maturity, the issuer of the bond, and not the dealer from whom the bond was purchased, redeems the bond and issues a cheque for the face value. There are no costs embedded into the redemption of the bond at maturity, nor are there any additional fees charged.

SUMMARY OF FEES AND COMMISSIONS

Banks, investment firms and mutual fund companies are businesses. They employ people, they have costs and they are expected to generate a profit for their shareholders. Canadian banks don't make billions of dollars every year by giving away their services. With every product or service there is a fee that is either obvious or embedded. Investors can pretend they aren't being charged if they don't see a fee but there is always a cost to do business.

The solution is to be aware of costs and ensure that they are fair. However, fixating solely on costs at the expense of all other aspects of planning and saving for retirement can be counterproductive.

Advisor Compensation

Most financial advisors are compensated on the revenue they generate through fees and commissions.

A typical investment dealer may keep 55% to 70% of commissions generated and pay the remainder to the advisor. The firm's share covers costs such as branch office overheads, a share of head office expenses, investment research costs and so on. The individual advisor often receives 30% to 45% of the total commissions generated. Their share of costs includes such items as licensing, advertising, marketing and sometimes a portion of their assistant's salary.

Notes:

- Fees and commission charges are not always transparent.
- Different commissions can apply to various investments.
- Management fees can be embedded in the price of a product without the investor realizing what the true costs are.
- There has been a movement towards greater transparency.
- Most advisors are paid a percentage of the fees and/or commissions collected.

CLIENT SERVICE AGREEMENT
(INVESTMENT POLICY STATEMENT)

A CLIENT SERVICE AGREEMENT is not a document that is required by regulators (at least not yet) but it can help form the basis of a strong relationship between an investor and their advisor. It establishes formal guidelines for managing a portfolio. The investor and advisor agree to the terms of the client service agreement and both sign the document.

It can be a simple or detailed document. It can include asset mix guidelines, income requirements, parameters for choosing individual investments, commission structure, the review process, the preferred method of communication and so on.

It can help the advisor narrow down suggestions for a client portfolio and it can also make the final decision less agonizing for the client. Investors can more easily see where everything fits, they know what the commission charges will be and they can have a lot more confidence that they are on the right track.

The great majority of investors probably don't have client service agreements but introducing a simplified document is a good first step. Some investors may eventually move to a more detailed agreement, while others may find a basic client service agreement to be sufficient.

Institutional accounts, such as pension plans and charitable organizations, use client service agreements or investment policy statements.

These agreements can be an important reference document in the event of a misunderstanding. The client and advisor can go back to the client service agreement and see what was agreed on by both parties. It becomes easier to resolve any disagreement.

It can also help clients keep their portfolios on track. Between the hype of the media and hot tips from colleagues, clients are often bombarded by investment ideas, each one seemingly better than the last. In this case, a client service agreement can provide discipline. If an investment doesn't fit within the guidelines agreed to by both parties it can be immediately eliminated, and if it does fit, the client service agreement can help clarify where it fits and how much is appropriate.

It may seem like a lot of work to develop such an agreement for your account; however, a foundation is being laid for a successful relationship between the client and the advisor. The golden rule of the financial services industry is "know your client" and the client service agreement is another tool which helps the advisor to know how the client wants his account to be managed.

The following is an example of information that might be included in a 'client service agreement'. These guidelines help to ensure that the advisor and the client are on the same page. It improves the level of knowledge that each party has with regard to the other and improved knowledge increases your chances of success and reduces the chances for a misunderstanding to occur.

You can also see an example of a basic client service agreement at: www.moneypages.ca

Account Management Guidelines

Purpose - The purpose of this document is to provide information on documenting, implementing, monitoring and evaluating your investment portfolio.

Client Service Agreement (Investment Policy Statement)

Time Horizon - Your time horizon is an important consideration and cyclical market fluctuations will be viewed with that perspective. Investors with short time horizons will have different needs than those with longer time horizons.

Risk Tolerance - Achieving your investment objectives will require that some risk be incurred. Historical data suggests that the risk of principal loss over a holding period of three years or longer can be reduced by the long term investment mix employed by the portfolio. You choose a risk level that you are comfortable with and this is listed in the client service agreement.

Asset Allocation - You and your advisor will select an asset allocation strategy designed to match your tolerance to risk and investments will be selected with that asset allocation as a guideline. Over time, your financial situation, objectives and tolerance to risk may change, so the appropriateness of the asset allocation strategy will be reviewed at least once every two years.

Mutual Fund Selection Process – Outline a process for selecting mutual funds. An example may be as follows: Mutual funds considered for the portfolio(s) will have a track record of at least three years. Track record of performance and volatility as compared to peers will be considered with written comments outlining the reasons for any such suggestions.

Equity and ETF Selection Process – Outline a process for selecting individual equities and ETFs. An example may be as follows: Individual equities and ETFs (exchange traded funds) considered for the portfolio will trade for above five dollars per share.

Fixed Income Selection Process - Outline a process for selecting individual bonds. An example may be as follows: Individual bonds considered for the portfolio will preferably have a credit rating of BBB or higher.

GIC Selection Process - Outline a process for selecting GICs. An example may be as follows: Investments with a single GIC issuer will be kept below $100,000 whenever possible. If the amount for investment exceeds $100,000 the use of GICs from multiple suppliers will be encouraged to maintain maximum CDIC coverage.

Portfolio Reviews – Outline the frequency of reviews (quarterly, semi-annually, annually) that you will have with your advisor and the topics that will be covered in the reviews.

Fees and Commissions – Outline any fees and commissions involved in managing your account. These fees include:

- Trading commissions for buying and/or selling equities and exchange traded funds.
- Mutual fund commissions, whether they are no load, front load, or back load; and what the redemption schedule might be, if applicable.
- Commissions charged for the purchase and/or sale of bonds.
- Transfer fees that might be charged for transferring your accounts to a new institution.
- Annual administration fees.
- Other applicable fees and commissions.

COMPLIANCE

Investment firms have *compliance departments* that monitor their advisors to ensure they are *complying with industry regulations*. In addition, full service investment dealers (those licensed to sell stocks, bonds and ETFs as well as mutual funds) typically must be members of the Investment Industry Regulatory Organization of Canada or IIROC.

IIROC's website is: www.iiroc.ca/

The reason it is important to discuss compliance is because the rules and regulations serve as protection, not against losing money on your investments, but against unscrupulous or fraudulent practices. They are also designed to prevent illegal practices, such as money laundering, from occurring.

As with any form of protection, there is a cost involved and a portion of the fees and commissions you pay are used to cover the cost of compliance.

One of the goals of compliance departments is to ensure portfolios are properly aligned to meet the client's needs and are managed in an appropriate manner. In order to accomplish this goal, the status of the clients' accounts is monitored to ensure the information is complete and up-to-date.

Some of the responsibility needs to fall upon the client to keep their documentation up-to-date. While regulators regard this as a vital requirement, many clients see it as an aggravation or an intrusion of their privacy. The documents can often sit unopened on the kitchen table for weeks without being completed and returned.

However, updates are a regulatory requirement that advisors and clients must comply with.

The consequences of not keeping documentation updated can result in trading restrictions. While the funds in your account will still be accessible, you may be prohibited by regulators from making changes to your investment portfolio or from making new investments.

Current legislation requires account objectives to be updated and confirmed every two or three years. It takes only a few minutes to review, update and sign the appropriate form to ensure that you and your financial advisor are on the same page. It is in everyone's best interests to remain onside with the regulatory requirements.

New legislation will require all investments to be ranked by the risk or volatility inherent in each particular investment. You will need to decide what percentage of your account is devoted to low risk, moderate risk and high risk investments.

The risk rankings of the individual investments are used in conjunction with your asset allocation to select a mix of investments that are most suitable for your financial situation.

The project was introduced in early 2013 and, as with any new undertaking, the process of ranking investments will evolve over time. While it is not a perfect system, the information gathered over time will help to improve the risk ranking process.

Online and discount brokers may not be obligated to provide you with a risk ranking on individual investments.

It is important to remember that these are efforts by the investment industry to assist you and your advisor in making decisions that best suit your needs and objectives. If you are uncertain, ask your advisor to demonstrate how their firm ranks investments.

SECTION SEVEN

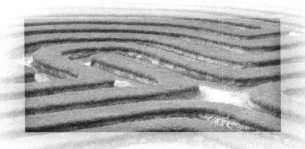

IMPLEMENTING YOUR PLAN & MANAGING YOUR PORTFOLIO

IMPLEMENTING YOUR PLAN

At the beginning of the book I indicated that many people hope to start down the road to financial success by selecting a specific investment. I will reiterate that it should be the last decision that is made. All of the other pieces need to be put into place first. Financial goals and tolerance to risk need to be identified, a plan put into place and an asset allocation chosen. Tax-free, tax deferred and taxable accounts need to be used to maximum benefit.

Once all of that is put into place, appropriate investments that meet your personal criteria can be chosen.

A Review of the Process

- Establish your financial goals.
- Determine your tolerance to risk.
- Develop a financial plan to achieve those goals.
- Choose an appropriate asset allocation.
- Implement your investment strategy by choosing investments that fit your asset allocation.

- Manage your portfolio.

INVESTMENT SELECTION

The selection of the specific investments within each asset class is a dynamic process because economic conditions can change quickly and dramatically. Suggesting investments in this book would be foolhardy. Before the ink was dry, many of the recommendations would be out-of-date.

There are those who suggest an approach where you invest in index funds where the content of those funds gives you a diversified portfolio that rarely changes. But applying a blanket (or index) approach does not always create the best results. Someone has to decide what is in the index and the people who make those decisions are not always infallible.

There are three good examples that contradict the index approach:

- Nortel represented about one-third of the value of the S&P/TSX Composite Index in September 2000. Today it is worthless.

- As of the end of 2012, Canada's broadest index had no exposure to the REIT sector in Canada. For the past ten years REITs have been one of the best performing sectors of the Canadian market.

- Gold bullion is virtually ignored by every index but it too has been one of the best performing asset classes for the past ten years.

In these cases, the index held a very large amount of one of the worst possible investments and completely ignored two strong performing asset classes. Don't automatically assume that choosing an index is the easy way to make a sound investment decision. Besides, there are hundreds of different indexes from which to choose and deciding which are appropriate is challenging.

Selecting appropriate investments is reliant on ever-changing economic and financial data. The decision should be made when you are ready to make the investment and not beforehand.

Implementing your plan — stage of life considerations

Everyone will be in their own unique situation when they begin the process of investing. Some will be in the early stages of their life, some in their high earning years, some close to retirement and some will already be retired. Regardless of what stage you are at, it is never too late to develop a plan. Exactly how you implement that plan will depend, in part, on what stage you are at.

Early Adult Period

Many advisors are happy to work with novice investors who are eager and willing to learn about what is required from a planning, investing and administrative point of view. Even novice investors should be diligent about their choice of advisors and using the criteria outlined earlier is a good place to begin.

Taking small steps and learning as you go helps build a base of knowledge that can be helpful later in life when you will probably have significantly more money available for investment. It can be a good time to learn all of this when only small amounts of money are involved. Poor markets or unfortunate decisions won't affect your long term financial future and lessons learned at this stage can be valuable later in life.

Those who are serious about undertaking even a small investment program and 'learning the ropes' should strongly consider an investment dealer that offers a full range of products, including mutual funds, exchange traded products and individual bonds.

The good news is that you can start with a very small account. At this level, investment choices are limited, but it is still worthwhile to start investing. You will begin accumulating savings and at the same time gain an understanding of the administrative requirements involved in beginning an investment program.

The benefits of starting early should not be underestimated. Take the example of two investors who expect to achieve a return of 6% per year on their investments. One begins their investment program at age 30 and one at age 45. Both have the goal of retiring at age 65 when they will begin to draw on their investments.

The investor who began at age 30 saves $6,000 per year while the investor who began at age 45 saves $18,000 per year. Both accumulate the same total savings by age 65. In 35 years the younger investor has set aside $210,000 ($6,000 x 35 years) while the older investor has had to save $360,000 ($18,000 x 20 years) to accomplish the same result.

In this example, by the time the 30 year old reaches age 45, he will have $12,000 more per year to spend on his lifestyle than the person who waited until 45 to begin his savings program.

While a balance between living for today and saving for tomorrow must be developed, it is clear that starting a savings plan earlier in life can have huge benefits, not only in retirement but in the years leading to retirement.

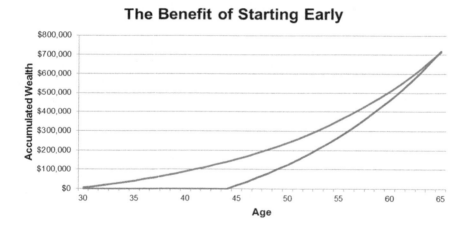

Begin with mutual funds

The easiest way to get your investment account started is to set up a pre-authorized chequing plan (or PAC plan). Each month on a specified date your bank account will be debited and those funds will be credited to your accounts. PAC plans work best with mutual funds; they are cumbersome and expensive if you are trying to buy stocks or ETFs.

You can also make lump sum mutual fund purchases in addition to your monthly pre-authorized chequing plan. Simply make a deposit into your investment account and decide, along with your advisor, which fund you want to purchase. There is no additional paperwork required and in many cases the transaction can be completed with a phone call.

Mutual funds provide access to a variety of asset classes including cash, fixed income, equities, REITs, precious metals and so on.

When getting started, the novice investor should complete the same risk tolerance questionnaire as a larger and more seasoned investor. The investments should then be made following those guidelines.

Accounts

The first thing you should do does not involve opening an account. You should pay down any debts you may have as quickly as possible. This may include student loans, car loans and making extra payments on your mortgage.

When considering which accounts to use, starting with a TFSA makes a lot of sense. Any growth within the account is tax-free and it can be withdrawn without incurring any tax liabilities. Since the financial situation of those who are in the early stages of their working careers can be volatile, the flexibility of a TFSA holds a lot of appeal.

The next account to consider is an RRSP account. Generally speaking, you will probably be in a lower income tax bracket in the early stages of your life and a higher income tax bracket as your career progresses. Contributing to an RRSP when your income is low does not generate great tax savings. You can delay those contributions to those years when your income is higher and get a larger tax benefit.

In the meantime, your investments can still grow tax-free in your TFSA and you won't lose your RRSP contribution room even if you don't take advantage of it immediately. The exception to this strategy applies to those who are earning a very high income early in their working careers. In that case, RRSP contributions will make sense.

The last account to consider is a taxable investment account. Even those with relatively large incomes may have little left after doubling on mortgage payments, making maximum TFSA contributions and maximizing their

RRSP contributions. For those who still have extra funds available, it is a good problem to have and a taxable investment account can be established.

Mid-Life Period

At this stage of your life you should have a greater capacity to save and invest than you did when you were younger. Hopefully, your debt load has decreased and your income has increased.

You will probably want to expand your investments beyond mutual funds to include exchange traded funds and individual investments. It is a good idea to continue with monthly contributions to your various accounts and supplement those with lump sum contributions when the opportunity arises.

You probably already have a TFSA and an RRSP in place. Maximizing your RRSP contributions makes a great deal of sense at this stage. You may be in the highest tax bracket of your working career and you will probably be in a lower tax bracket upon retirement. The theory is that you create the maximum tax benefit with your RRSP contribution but pay tax at a much lower rate when you begin to withdraw in retirement.

Your available contribution limits are easily found on the *Notice of Assessment* you receive from the Canada Revenue Agency (CRA). That document usually arrives in May or June after you have filed your tax return. It is a good time to make your RRSP contribution and maximize it if possible.

TFSA Accounts

The program began in 2009 for those who are eighteen years of age or older. As of 2013 the annual contribution limits were increased to $5,500 per year while the maximum lifetime contribution limit stood at $25,500. Contributions to your TFSA account should be maximized before making any contributions to a taxable investment account.

Those who have taxable investment accounts but have not yet contributed to a TFSA should immediately open a TFSA and transfer the maximum amount allowable into that account. In many cases, you can simply transfer existing investments to a TFSA and immediately cease paying taxes on the growth generated.

Your taxable investments

Many Canadians will find it challenging to take full advantage of the contribution limits provided by their RRSP accounts and their TFSA accounts. Those who still have additional funds to invest can consider a taxable investment account.

Because income tax will apply on gains on your investments, it is important to consider how the gains provided by various investments will be taxed.

While interest is the most predictable form of return, it is also taxed at the highest rate. Dividends are less certain than interest but the tax benefits make them worth considering. The least certain form of return is capital gain, but once again, tax considerations and the potential for higher returns can make the pursuit of capital gains attractive.

PRE-RETIREMENT AND RETIREMENT PERIOD

In retirement your primary focus will shift from growth on your investments to income generated from your investments. RRSP accounts will likely be converted to RRIF accounts so you can begin to draw income from those accounts.

Income can be drawn for your tax-free savings accounts as well as your taxable investment accounts. If you still do not have a tax-free savings account but have money in taxable investment or savings accounts, you should immediately open a tax-free savings account and contribute as much as is allowed.

In subsequent years you should continue to move as much as possible from your taxable investment accounts to your tax-free savings accounts. Unlike RRSP accounts, there is no age limit for contributions; investors who are in their 90s can still make contributions. The reason behind this strategy is that a larger and larger portion of your investment income will become non-taxable each year.

Another overlooked advantage of TFSAs is that you can name a beneficiary so the proceeds bypass probate. This feature makes TFSAs a useful estate planning tool and reduces the need for segregated funds in estate planning.

Tax considerations

In a taxable investment account dividends can provide a significant advantage over interest. For one thing, dividends are taxed at a lower rate than interest. A 5% return via dividends is much better than a 5% return via interest in a taxable account.

Dividends can actually reduce your taxes, as shown in the following example:

> *Let's take the example of a 67 year old Ontario resident who collects $6,000 per year in OAS benefits, $9,000 per year in CPP benefits, withdraws $12,000 from their RIF and earns $8,000 per year in interest income. Their total income would be $35,000 and they would have paid approximately $3,800 in taxes in 2011. Net income would have been about $31,200.*
>
> *If that same investor had earned $8,000 in dividends rather than interest, taxes would have dropped to approximately $2,100 and after tax income would have been about $32,900. That represents a savings of about 40% on taxes payable.*

A website that allows you to plug in various scenarios and compare the results is www.taxtips.ca. Investments that pay dividends include high quality common shares as well as preferred shares.

MANAGING YOUR PORTFOLIO

MANAGING YOUR INVESTMENTS is not about trying to incorporate every good idea that you hear about into your portfolio. Following that path leads to a portfolio that has drifted away from your original objectives and often becomes concentrated in equities. Managing your investments is about making adjustments that fall within the guidelines that you have established for yourself.

If a stock seems to present an attractive opportunity and your portfolio is already at its maximum equity exposure, then you must decide which of your existing equities should be replaced by this new stock. That decision should be based not only on the potential performance of the new investment but also on its correlation with other investments in the portfolio. Keep the concept of diversification in mind.

Conversely, if an investment that you hold seems to be performing poorly, consider any changes carefully. For example, investors may be tempted to reduce their exposure to bonds dramatically when equity markets are in a strong uptrend. They begin to chase returns and abandon the concept of diversification and sound portfolio management.

While there can be a strong temptation to abandon an investment plan, if you have laid out a sound framework and honestly assessed your tolerance to risk, stick with your plan. If something still seems wrong, review your plan to ensure that your circumstances and objectives haven't changed dramatically. If they have, revise your plan before making any dramatic investment decisions.

There will be times when your portfolio will disappoint you and times when it will exceed expectations. It is important that you manage your portfolio in both of these situations.

Common mistakes

Two common mistakes that investors make when managing their finances are ignoring their portfolios and micromanaging their portfolios.

Ignoring your portfolio

When markets are performing poorly there is a natural human tendency to put the entire issue out of our minds.

No one likes bad news but leaving your statements unopened is a bad strategy. Investors who face adversity and make sound decisions in time of crisis are more likely to succeed. It might include a reevaluation of their tolerance to risk, a reallocation among asset classes or changes to specific investments.

Keep the lines of communication with your advisor open. Analyze the situation together and look for solutions rather than looking for someone to blame.

Micromanaging your portfolio

At the other end of the spectrum is the investor who micromanages his portfolio. It can become a case of not seeing the forest for the trees.

These investors agonize over day to day, week to week and month to month fluctuations in portfolio values. They want to act on every new idea they see and become impatient when portfolio performance lags even over short periods of time. Statements are compared every month and a short term drop in value suggests to them there is a flawed investment strategy or an impending crisis.

Micromanaging rarely leads to reducing volatility and will often reduce performance because of the additional costs incurred when making those changes. The results of this approach are reflected in the Dalbar report discussed earlier.

The Compromise

The best compromise is to honestly assess your tolerance to risk and build your portfolio with that as your guideline. You will still experience periods of time where your portfolio falls in value but a well-constructed portfolio should give you the confidence that your investments are well positioned.

That doesn't mean your portfolio should be put on cruise control. Conditions are always changing, unexpected risks may arise and unexpected opportunities may present themselves. Sound portfolio management takes those factors into consideration and makes appropriate adjustments within the guidelines you have set for yourself.

Notes:

- Mutual funds represent an effective way for small investors to start a diversified portfolio.

- Tax free savings accounts (TFSAs) provide another valuable tool for Canadians to grow their personal wealth.

- The type of account most appropriate for your situation will likely change over the course of your life.

- Taxes can have a significant impact on your efforts to accumulate wealth. Ensure that the accounts and the investments you choose take this into consideration.

- Your plan should be dynamic rather than static. It should change as your needs and your personal circumstances change.

SECTION EIGHT

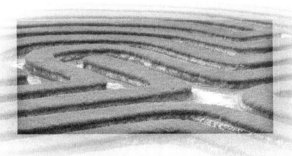

SUMMARY

SUMMARY

The task of managing our money throughout our lives is not a simple one. Along the way choices have to be made and priorities need to be set. Very few of these are easy.

Part of the problem is that many of your professional advisors may be focused on their particular area of expertise rather than the overall picture. The banker wants to lend you as much money as you can afford to pay back, the insurance representative wants to sell you as much insurance as possible, the realtor wants you to buy the most expensive house you can afford, the accountant wants you to adopt tax-driven strategies and the financial advisor wants you to save every nickel for retirement.

Given all of these conflicting approaches, it is a challenge to develop a comprehensive strategy that addresses all of these issues with a sense of balance. There are the lucky few whose careers or financial position allow these decisions to be pushed to the back of their minds without much worry. For the rest of us it takes some planning.

Financial Plan

It begins with a budget, or more accurately, budgets. These budgets do not need to be financial straitjackets, but they can help provide you with some direction and help identify where your money should be going.

Your budget during your working years can help you find ways to develop a savings plan that will result in an investment portfolio to fund your retirement. Your (future) retirement budget gives you the information you need to begin setting targets for retirement dates and the assets you will need to accumulate.

As you begin your savings and investment program, a process of self-examination is required. The task is to determine what kind of investor you are. In other words, how much volatility can you stand or, put another way, how much volatility is appropriate for your situation? It is something only you can determine, but there is help available.

The amount of assets you will need to accumulate along with your risk-tolerance profile will determine how much you will need to invest and how it should be invested.

The question of how your money should be invested is frequently the first question asked. In fact, many investors ask for opinions on specific investments without knowing whether or not those kinds of investments are even appropriate for their situation.

Throughout our lives our financial situation changes and our plans to address each of these unique situations need to be flexible. It is a good idea to have objectives in mind for each stage of our lives. Work with your financial advisor so you can develop a strategy to meet your objectives and then cross them off your list once they have been achieved.

Investment Plan

After identifying your risk tolerance profile, the next step is to identify, in broad terms, what kinds of investments should be held in your portfolio and in what proportions they should be held. This is the process of asset allocation. The broad categories of asset classes include cash, fixed income, preferred shares, real estate, equities and precious metals.

Only after determining what percentage of your portfolio should be held in each asset class should specific investments within each asset class be explored.

Generally speaking, your mix of investments (asset allocation) should remain relatively constant from one year to the next with only minor variations to account for changing economic conditions. Over time and as you approach retirement the asset allocation should gradually reflect a more conservative risk-tolerance profile.

Along the way it is important to monitor your progress to ensure that you are accumulating the capital that you will require to fund your retirement. While monitoring your rate of return can tell you if you have gained or lost ground over a given period of time, these results are often used in the wrong way. It is important to keep the rate of return achieved in perspective and relative to the world markets and economies.

Mistakes can be made in trying to compensate for periods of below average or negative returns. The wrong approach is to become significantly more aggressive than your risk-tolerance profile indicates is appropriate. The right approach is to increase contributions to your portfolio until you are back on-side. It doesn't have to be a lump sum and you don't have to catch up in one year, but you do need to adjust your savings patterns.

That means making some sacrifices in other areas and it is something our society has become unaccustomed to doing. As a society we always seem to looking for the easy to way to lose weight, get in shape and gain wealth. Given the number of infomercials on television, someone is taking the bait but a quick look around shows us that very few are following through.

It is worthwhile to examine the actual steps required to implement your plan. I recommend that you use a financial advisor to guide you through the process, assist you in structuring your accounts to provide maximum benefit, take care of the day-to-day administration requirements and provide you with financial advice; then it is helpful to know what to expect when starting that relationship.

Financial Advisor

Financial advisors tend to use their own unique approach to help clients manage their money. Some like to concentrate on helping their clients plan for retirement and build portfolios that will serve their needs over the long term. Others have a shorter term focus and prefer a trading strategy. Choose one whose style is compatible with what you are trying to accomplish.

Accounts

Once you have found an advisor you will need to decide what kinds of accounts best suit your needs. There are basically three types of accounts. These include taxable accounts, which are sometimes referred to as cash accounts, margin accounts or investment accounts; there are tax-deferred accounts, such as RRSP and RRIF accounts; and finally, there are tax-free accounts, or TFSA accounts, now available.

Your advisor can help you make those choices and help you to allocate appropriate resources to each.

Documentation

When you are first establishing your accounts a great deal of paperwork can be required if you are opening the account. This paperwork serves two purposes. It fulfills the requirement of the regulatory and government agencies and it also provides the advisor with the basic information required to properly understand your situation. Accurate and detailed information leads to the best recommendations and advice possible.

Once the paperwork is in place, dealing with an IIROC (Investment Industry Regulatory Organization of Canada) firm can be very convenient. Most business can be transacted over the phone. Because you are dealing with a specific advisor, you will almost always be talking to the same individuals regarding questions about your account. They will have an understanding of your situation and communications should be consistent and clear.

Regulations do require a brief update of your account information every two or three years to ensure that your advisor still has an accurate profile of your situation.

Fees and commissions

Before making the final commitment, know what fees and commissions apply to your various accounts and any transactions. It can be convoluted and it is better to have that information ahead of time to avoid any unpleasant surprises.

Investment policy statements

Investment policy statements (or client service agreements) formalize the agreement between you and your advisor. They provide guidelines with respect to portfolio construction, fees or commission and the portfolio review process. These agreements can be basic or detailed and can help to avoid any misunderstandings between you and your advisor.

Compliance

In a world that seems to be increasingly run by lawyers, prepare yourself for even more regulation. While these regulations may seem cumbersome and intrusive, they are designed to protect the rights of investors. The best course of action is to comply with the regulations. If you feel they are either lacking or unnecessary, make your thoughts known to the appropriate regulators. In the meantime, it is the environment in which clients and advisors must work.

Insurance

The role of life insurance needs to be examined and just as our investment needs change over time, so do our insurance needs. For most people, insurance should be just that...insurance. The exception can be very high net worth individuals who may have redundant capital (money they will not need to generate income for future living expenses). For them, advanced life insurance strategies can be employed that will complement investment programs. For most of us, these kinds of life insurance policies are forced savings that have significant costs associated with them and offer little value.

Other forms of insurance, such as long term disability, critical illness and long term care should be investigated to determine whether they suit your situation.

Just as some financial advisors may use the best case scenario when making investment presentations, some insurance agents use the worst case scenario to encourage insurance sales that may not be entirely necessary. Take the time to understand your insurance needs along with the costs and benefits of any policies.

Home Ownership

The decision to rent or buy a home is a personal one. In reality, it is more about making a lifestyle choice than about creating wealth. A large home doesn't necessarily create wealth and, in fact, home ownership can be so costly that it undermines your attempts to accumulate wealth and can cramp your lifestyle in the meantime.

Know all of the facts before jumping into buying a home in the misplaced belief that if you wait too long it will become unaffordable.

High Risk Strategies

While some strategies are obviously risky, there are others that may appear to be relatively conservative at first glance but actually belong in the high risk category. Promises of high returns or big tax savings can be tempting. Proceed with caution when something appears too good to be true.

Miscellaneous

The trend is toward making us more reliant on our own savings and investments in retirement. The days of future generations funding our golden years are slowly changing and we need to be prepared to look after ourselves.

Despite what you may read in the financial press or see on television, it will not be a simple or straightforward journey. Economic upheavals, political change, market corrections and unfortunate personal decisions can all be obstacles to our success. We can try to mitigate the effects of those incidents but there are no guarantees.

Your best protection doesn't come in the form of government guaranteed investments; it comes from building a sound plan and sticking to it as closely as possible; it comes from having the ability to adjust when things don't unfold as expected; it comes from being prepared.

CONCLUSION

Treating your money well is a key to financial success. It involves creating a vision, developing a plan and investing wisely. It involves being well-prepared and taking a logical approach to your personal finances rather than blindly following the next good idea.

There is always someone willing to tell you that there is a simple, painless solution to achieving personal wealth and a life of leisure. For a lucky few, that may be the case, but managing your personal finances is an ongoing process that requires personal discipline. The majority of us need to plan wisely, spend carefully, and save regularly.

The information in this book provides you with information and strategies to help you get started. If it seems too complicated to tackle on your own, don't throw up your hands in despair. I advocate the use of a financial advisor and have given you the tools to help you identify the individual who best suits your needs.

For many, the investment experience may be a new one. For others, the entire process may seem a little vague and confusing. This book demystifies the process of opening an account, preparing a financial plan and making investment decisions. It outlines the less than transparent fee structure that seems to be a characteristic of the investment industry and helps you make educated decisions on the products and services you choose.

Don't procrastinate. Take control of your personal finances and decide on a course of action.

Your best course of action may be to do it yourself based on your past experience, courses you may have taken and information you have gleaned from this book and others. Or you may choose to work with a financial advisor who can help you navigate through the world of finance.

Hopefully, in reading the chapters in this book, you have garnered numerous ideas that will help you in your efforts. Good luck!

I welcome your feedback. Please check our website www.moneymaze.ca and send your comments.

FEEDBACK

QUESTIONS

SPEAKING ENGAGEMENTS

CONTACT THE AUTHOR AT:
BOB.TRASK@MONEYMAZE.CA

CPSIA information can be obtained at www.ICGtesting.com
Printed in the USA
LVOW01s1922120214